Making
a Church from
Scratch

From Appointment to Charter—
The Story of Highland Hope

TROY BENITONE

MAKING A CHURCH FROM SCRATCH

© 1998 by Troy D. Benitone
Published by Bristol Books, an imprint of Bristol House, Ltd.

First Edition, December 1998

Unless otherwise indicated, all Scripture quotations are from the *Holy Bible, New International Version,* © 1973, 1978, 1984 by the International Bible Society. Used by permission of Zondervan Publishing House.

All rights reserved. Except for brief quotations embodied in critical articles and reviews, no part of this book may be used or reproduced in any manner whatsoever without written permission.

ISBN: 1-885224-18-4

Printed in the United States of America

Bristol House, Ltd.
P.O. Box 4020
Anderson, Indiana 46013-0020
Phone: 765-644-0856
Fax: 765-622-1045

To order call: 1-800-451-READ (7323)

A WORD OF THANKS

THIS BOOK WAS INSPIRED:

by my parents, Jerry and Donna, who raised me to be a dreamer and a risk-taker

by my grandparents, Don and Mayme Benitone, who encouraged me as a child to open my heart to Christ and the Church

by my wife, Beth, and my kids, Heather, Joshua, Caleb and Megan, who are gifts from God that make my life and ministry complete

by the encouragement of my best friend, Shane, and his wife, Melissa, who spoke up at the perfect time—twice

and, above all else, by God, who has given me awesome opportunities to serve

BLESSINGS AND LOVE
~
TO ALL OF YOU—HOPE IS ALIVE!
~
TROY

TABLE OF CONTENTS

FOREWORD.......................... 5

    THE RECIPE: You Can't Bake a
Church without a Recipe 9

    GETTING STARTED: The Utensils
and Cookware You Need 21

    STEP ONE: Start with Good Flour,
Crack Two Eggs, Add Milk and
Mix Thoroughly 47

    STEP TWO: Add Yeast and
Let Rise!............................. 65

    STEP THREE: Punch It Down 73

    STEP FOUR: Let It Rise Again!....... 79

    STEP FIVE: Form It into a Loaf 91

    STEP SIX: Glaze with Olive Oil 99

    THE TASTE TEST: Let Cool
and Charter/Serve..................... 107

HINTS: APPENDIX: Some Tips
    from the Chef 115

FOREWORD

One of my greatest loves in life is cooking. I come from an Italian family which has given me a genetic capacity to cook from scratch. Rev. Chuck Carpenter, my CPE (Clinical Pastoral Education) supervisor, once told me, *"You have olive oil running through those veins."*

Cooking for me is not an exact science; it is sort of like an episode of Justin Wilson's *Homecooking*. I don't measure; I season, salt and cook to taste. However, one of my greatest kitchen endeavors is baking fresh Italian bread—the one delicacy that requires a recipe. Without a recipe, the bread's taste, texture and presentation are never consistent.

Another calling of mine is developing new churches or church planting, as some call it. In pursuing these two disciplines—baking and church planting—I have found some striking similarities that provide the structure for this treatise—a recipe.

Whether you are interested in developing a new worship service aimed at a specific target group of unchurched people in your community, or you are considering relocating your existing church to a new location and have the opportunity to make a new beginning, or your bulging congregation has aspirations of starting a second campus/satellite church or helping to plant a sister church, or you are the pastor sent to the community of X—this recipe is for you.

In 1990 God called me into pastoral ministry, setting a fire in my heart and spirit to do the work of an apostle, to be about the work of building new communities of faith that will meet the needs of the Christian family. A spiritual mentor of mine, Rev. Fred Bishop, director of a Christian men's leadership outreach ministry called No Greater Love Ministries, taught me that to fulfill your heart's desire and calling requires one to "Study to show thyself approved unto God . . ." as Scripture mandates (2 Timothy 2:15, KJV). In all things we must pay our dues by going through a time as an apprentice, then becoming a journeyman and finally becoming a craftsman.

Over the next four years I began my apprentice work as a part-time local pastor in two small United Methodist Churches in southern Illinois. In that first appointment, I found the life lessons the parishioners taught me to be much greater than what I was preaching to them.

During my apprenticeship, despite my failures and faults, these two churches experienced above average growth, not only in membership but, more importantly, in attendance. Best of all, many people were converted to Christ and baptized. In addition, many came to know God as a Sanctifier.

How did this transformation start? A few hard shells yielded to the Holy Spirit. A few people received the gift of healing. Others were simply prime for the harvest. I became a witness to the scriptural precept, *". . . if I [Jesus] be lifted up from the earth I will draw all [people] unto me"* (John 12:32, KJV). When Christ is preached, we can expect what the world calls the supernatural to be natural. I knew that if a church could grow and prosper in a small town like Energy or Colp, then southern Illinois was "white already to harvest" (John 4:35, KJV). Through that movement of God the seed he had planted in my heart began to grow.

I moved on to Atlanta, Georgia, to complete my apprenticeship as a student at Emory University in the Candler School of Theology and as a student pastor to two small South Georgia churches in Manchester. While at Candler, I found church development to be far from the agenda of the typical colloquy discussion. However, I did receive inspiration from two distinguished Wesleyan theologians. Not only were these professors an inspiration, but they provided me with the stories, lessons and examples from their lectures, the story of their lives and their experience to change my life tremendously. Bishop William J. Canon and Bishop W. T. Handy[1] both have the heart and mind of true Wesleyans. They talked of "saving souls," "holiness of heart and life," "building the kingdom of God," and "being about the Great Commission."

In Bishop W. T. Handy's class called "Evangelizing the Church," we were given the opportunity to visit some of the fastest-growing churches in Atlanta and to meet with the leadership and find out about their plans and visions for ministry. Bishop Handy not only had us experience these great churches first hand, he had class groups share reports, so by the end of the class we had received and experienced an in-depth presentation of each of these successful church growth models. Bishop Handy also brought in a pastor of a declining church so that we might examine, review and note the signs and issues surrounding a failing parish. Bishop Handy was not scared to ask tough questions about why some churches, pastors and ministries become ineffective.

---

[1] Bishop William J. Canon went to be with God on May 11, 1997. Bishop W. T. Handy, Jr. went to be with God on Easter Sunday, April 12, 1998.

These bishops reminded us that there is always hope and there is always a place for pastors with vision and enthusiasm. What it will take is bishops, cabinet members and church leaders exercising wisdom and discernment, leaders who are determined to make the kingdom of God first priority in utilizing these pastors effectively. I enjoyed the stories Bishop Handy shared with our class about young pastors he had appointed and the great things God did. In short, these men gave me hope.

I left Candler in July, 1994, heading for Illinois once again, to serve as the associate at Olney Immanuel UMC, the home of the white squirrels (the area is famous for its rare albino squirrels, which are coddled and protected by local residents). Initially, I could not figure out why in God's creation Illinois Area Bishop David J. Lawson, in his infinite wisdom, would send me to Olney Immanuel United Methodist Church. I was not a white squirrel groupie, and that initially seemed to be the community's only drawing card. Upon meeting the senior pastor of Immanuel, the Rev. Dr. Bruce F. Owens, I quickly understood. Dr. Owens held a Doctorate of Ministry in Church Development. You see, very few clergy hold doctorates of any sort in my small conference of some 395 churches,[2] let alone one with the training, insight and experiences of Dr. Owens. Dr. Owens was a true Wesleyan with the tenacity and training of a NAVY Sea Bee, as he served in the Navy during Vietnam.

My time at Immanuel was to be as a journeyman. From day one Dr. Owens invited me to be creative and gave me complete freedom and support in working with the programming for ages 40 and under. In this time I developed an effective children's ministry program that included a complete remodeling of the nursery, a children's church, a successful after-school kids club program (inherited from my predecessor), a 5th–6th grade Young Life group, a Jr.–Sr. High UMYF, a high school music and drama ministry and a special High School Youth Focus study group. An adult program called "Body, Soul & Spirit!" was designed to attract adults ages 18–40 and included activities such as Christian low-impact aerobics and softball for the body, a Christian family movie night for the soul, and Home Serendipity Groups to develop the spirit.

During the year I was at Olney, things went by like a blur. The church came alive with youth and young adults, and the ministry was vibrant and growing. I now understand the need to be a journeyman.

---

[2] This statistic comes from the former Southern Illinois Conference, now a part of the new Illinois Great Rivers Conference, formed August 17, 1996 from the merger of the Southern Illinois and Central Illinois Conference. They now represent approximately 1,011 churches.

Have you ever been to the circus and seen the men and women on the flying trapeze? Don't think they began with those daring acts. When they are learning, their training begins by working at low levels with simple tasks. They do a lot of watching and learning from skilled and proven performers. As they get better, they go up to the higher swings, and a big safety net is placed under them so when they slip and fall they are lightly reminded that the key to success is practice, prayer and patience. If all of these great men and women of the circus practiced without a net, there would be no Ringling Brothers. This is why God sent me to Olney.

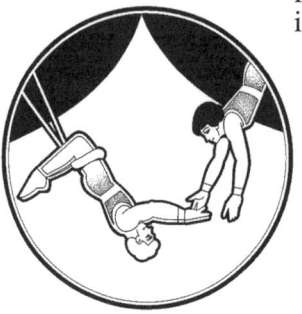

> **HAVE YOU EVER BEEN TO THE CIRCUS AND SEEN THE MEN AND WOMEN ON THE FLYING TRAPEZE?**

Despite the success I was achieving and the great vision and leadership that Dr. Owens was providing, I learned one of the fundamental lessons of church growth: the enemy, the devil,[3] does not care for church growth and lies in wait for those who champion it. I watched Dr. Owens champion his vision dozens of times, and he taught me that sometimes the safest approach was with our backs to one another. I learned that to be successful, effective and lasting in the area of church development and growth, to be on the frontline of the kingdom of God, to stand against the very enemy of God, I would need the support of a strong and loving Christian spouse and family, faithful colleagues, mentors and friends, the determination of a Navy Sea Bee and the unending, unmerited, unstoppable, infinite grace of God.

After only one year, I received a call by my district superintendent. The ministry that God had started me toward in 1990 had arrived. I would be the pastor of a new church in Highland, Illinois, effective July, 1995. I jumped for joy! Then I swallowed deeply, realizing the circus master was removing the net.

Troy Benitone

---

[3] Normal rules of grammar have been intentionally ignored in the capitalization of proper names referring to the devil, the enemy or satan, so as to give no glory or proper place within this text.

THE RECIPE:
YOU CAN'T BAKE A CHURCH WITHOUT A RECIPE

INTRODUCING THE SUBJECT OF THIS BOOK

Making a Church from Scratch is the story of Highland Hope and how one church was started. This is not a book on how to start a church, but, rather, a book on how one *can* be started. There is no way to tell anyone how to start a church. "How to" depends on the people, the place, the time, the sponsor churches, the resolve of the conference and many other factors. But, ultimately, it comes down to God's will and how this fits within the plans of the great I AM. I hope that pastors, laity and churches with an interest in church growth can catch some vision and glimpse some possibilities in my experiences, gleaning ideas that might work in their own various settings.

THE PERSPECTIVE

This book is not about a conference's vision to start a church, or the cabinet and bishop's resolve to begin a new church. Rather, this book is about one pastor's vision to be a church planter. In no way do I underestimate the importance of the annual conference and cabinets' resolve to start new churches and their vision and commitment to do so. I thank God for the vision of all the parties involved, which shows that great things can be accomplished when the body of Christ works together. However, this story focuses on the pastor's calling, the methodology used and the lessons learned.

The early apostles and disciples traveled in pairs as they journeyed abroad to minister. This custom was passed to the early founders of Methodism. John Wesley rode some 250,000 horseback miles through Europe and was often accompanied by colleagues and ministers of the faith. It was the custom of the first circuit riders, as with our first bishops, Thomas Coke and Francis Asbury, to ride through the parishes and districts of the early American Methodist Church of the 1780s. They would be joined by the traveling elder assigned to that location. Together they would discuss theological insights, homiletical tips and strategic plans as they traversed the fruited plains of early America.

In the same tradition, the vision of Highland Hope, from my perspective, started when I was first called into the ministry in the early spring of 1990. The plan began to take an identifiable form in the spring of 1995 when my best friend and colleague in the ministry and I traveled together in a car across the state of Illinois to look over the town of Highland. The cabinet of the Southern Illinois Conference had appointed me to begin a church there later that year, beginning July 1, 1995. In that car, Rev. Shane Bishop and I talked about our callings, dreams and visions. We prayed together over what the church in Highland would be named. We played with lots of names like grace, and other names that go with fellowship and chapel. We looked at maps and sought out the names of creeks, valleys, streets and hills. We even tried names that go with the county name. We tried saints' names, first church names, second and even third church names. We tried the names of famous Methodist leaders and locations. We even sank so low as to try "The First Church of Rev. Troy D. Benitone," but we thought some might consider me vain. Imagine that!

All the goofy word play made our trip that day seem like a page from the famous Dr. Seuss story *The Cat in the Hat*. But my heart jumped as we settled on a word that sits in the company of the three most precious qualities described in Scripture: "And now these three remain: faith, hope and love" (1 Corinthians 13:13). Faith is how we take God's hand, in hope we walk with God and trust in the Christ's returning and in love we begin to understand God's purpose and desire for all, which is for us to love God and each other. We settled on the name "Hope." We felt that our lost and dying world needs hope more than anything else. We also felt this name would create a strong positive image in the minds of today's baby boomers, busters and generation Xers,[1] all of whom need and seek hope and love.

The Scripture that spoke to me in the light of this need says *"But in your hearts set apart Christ as Lord. Always be prepared to give an answer to everyone who asks you to give the reason for the hope that you have. But do this with gentleness and respect"* (1 Peter 3:15).

Thus we named the unborn church "Highland Hope."

THE NEED

Highland Hope was born of a vision and calling that God set in my heart to be involved in the ministry of planting new churches. This calling was united with a conference and cabinet resolved to seek a new vision for the future. Why? The statistical reports of the former Southern Illinois Conference over the last 25 years reveal a steady and uninterrupted decline in the membership of our conference. The atrophy is incredible. As of 1996 we were 27.73% smaller than we were in 1972. (See Table 1 for statistics of the Southern Illinois Conference over the last 25 years. Unfortunately, these statistics also are typical of the decline in other United Methodist conferences.)

How did I come to study these gruesome details? While at a conference on New Church Development led by the General Board, I asked the question, "Why are we losing members? Has anyone done an in-

---

[1] Throughout the book I refer often to these three groups which, for the most part, the church has lost contact with. They are the baby boomers, busters and generation X (Xers is my abbreviation). Baby boomers include those born from 1943–1960; they are the children of the war era of World War II and Korea. The baby busters were born from 1961–1970 and are the children of older boomer parents. These kids grew up in the age of Vietnam; their parents were probably at or know someone who went to Woodstock. Xers were born between 1970–1981 and are the kids of younger boomers and busters. They have been raised on MTV, Nintendo, day care, and two-income families. These are not exact or complete descriptions of these groups, but you can find a lot of information about them elsewhere. If you are going to start ministries that reach out to people in these groups, you will need to read, meet, talk and develop an understanding of these unique generational cultures.

TABLE 1
Southern Illinois Conference Vital Signs

A Look at the Vital Signs of the Southern Illinois Conference (Statistics taken from Conference journals)

Year	1972	1973	1989	1990	1994	1995	1996	Totals
How did we gain members?								
Confession of faith	1532	1442	971	1273	1228	1212	1136	
Transferred from other UM churches	1025	911	647	671	565	519	591	
Transferred from other denominations	416	398	486	486	407	495	456	
How did we lose members?								
Removed by Charge Conference action	-2150	-1178	-1131	-1285	-1169	-1189	-1162	
Transferred to other UM churches	-1156	-1044	-626	-610	-537	-502	-510	
Transferred to other churches	-455	-401	-348	-359	-335	-312	-276	
By death	-1082	-991	-975	-1001	-971	-955	-921	
Net loss or gain	-1870	-863	-976	-25	-812	-732	-686	
Total loss of membership	-4843	-3614	-3080	-3255	-3012	-2958	-2869	
Analysis								
% loss due to death	22.34%	27.42%	31.66%	30.75%	32.24%	32.29%	32.10%	29.83%
% loss to transfers to other UM churches	23.87%	28.89%	20.32%	18.74%	17.83%	16.97%	17.78%	20.63%
Total unpreventable losses:	46.21%	56.31%	51.98%	49.49%	50.07%	49.26%	49.88%	50.46%
% loss to Charge Conference action	44.29%	32.60%	36.72%	39.48%	38.81%	40.20%	40.50%	38.96%
% loss to other churches	9.50%	11.10%	11.30%	11.03%	11.12%	10.55%	9.62%	10.59%
Total preventable losses	53.79%	43.69%	48.02%	50.51%	49.93%	50.74%	50.12%	49.54%

Total Southern Illinois Conference membership as of January 1, 1972 = 72,998
Total Southern Illinois Conference membership as of December 31, 1995 = 52,756
Total loss of membership from 1972–1995 (total 25 years) = 20,252
Total loss of membership as a percentage of the 1972 base = 27.73%

depth exit interview with any one of the 60,000 persons who left the United Methodist Church this year or the quarter of a million that left in the last four-year quadrennium?" The reply was, "No!" I was shocked.

As an insurance and securities broker, running my own business, I had faced ups and downs. When business was down, I reviewed my services, my products, my staffing and my presentation. I analyzed everything to discover how to effectively increase sales. When a client canceled their policy I always, even though I hated to hear the answer, asked "Why?" Of course, some business losses I could not prevent as people died or moved out of the area. Some fell upon hard times and could no longer afford my services. But if I was no longer competitive and they simply took their business to a local competitor, or decided the product was not worth the investment or were unhappy with my service—these things I could fix or at least become aware of. Then I would dedicate my energies to resolving this deficit.

While the church is not in the business of insurance sales, we are in the business of commissioned sales, taking the Great Commission abroad and sharing it with a world in need of God. When I asked my question, one of the conference leaders stared at me with eyes that could kill, as if I were terribly out of line for daring to question why our church is wasting away. He defensively responded that there would be numerous reasons, "too many to be of any use."

I said, "Fine. We can tackle them one at a time from the highest to lowest priority."

He replied, "But, see, we're not really losing members. They're just dying, and it's ATTRITION."

I responded, "It's not attrition, it's MALNUTRITION."

However, at that time I was not prepared to argue further. I went home and, as I had done so many times in my insurance days, did my homework. Pulling out conference journals from the last 25 years, I found that 50% of the 20,252 persons our conference had lost over the last 25 years could be categorized as "preventable" losses. Of the total losses, 38.96% were charged off like a business writes off bad debts, dropped by Charge Conference action. Some say this is unpreventable, but each of these people at some point in time, whether they remained faithful for one day or 20 years, stood up before a United Methodist congregation and a United Methodist pastor and was received into the membership of the church. Remember, when we perform the service of receiving members into the church not only do they join us, but we join them. We become connected to them in a covenantal and "connectional" manner. Over the years I have seen dozens of divorces, and there has not been one case where one side was completely without fault. I imagine in each of these cases of lost members a welcoming and warmer smile, some personal attention, a lay person's invitation to lunch or out to get a cup of coffee, a person sliding over in the pew they have sat in for 20 years and inviting a new person to find a seat next to them, might have resulted in a different outcome.

The records show that 27.73% of us have disappeared, leaving 72.27%—a mere shadow of our former selves. Where will this end? Can a body survive with 1/3, 1/2, 3/4 or 9/10 of its members gone? By nature, a covenant binds us to these people. We have a responsibility. Even though many of our leaders, members and pastors stick their heads in the sand, the fact is we are on a terminal path that leads to certain death. Many conferences throughout Methodism are merging and reorganizing. Even the 1996 General Conference passed sweeping reform to downsize and simplify committees. Why? Because we're dying!

Some 10 percent of our conference's losses have been to other denominations and independent churches. Why have so many had a loss of heart and faith in our church? Maybe, no longer is "the main thing, the main thing" in our congregations. Too often we try to say, "Everything is the best thing." I only wish this were true, but the Word says "I am the main Way, the True thing, the only Life, and there is nothing beyond Jesus Christ" (my paraphrase of John 14:6). Maybe we need to investigate where we have made mistakes and what we are selling today.

What about the preventable losses? What about the other half, the 50 percent of "preventable" losses that have left our flock? It is a fact that 50 percent of our declining membership is a result of unpreventable circumstances. As we all know, the circle of life ends in death. But—does it? A circle is a circle, not a dead end. The circle of life reveals that baby boomers, busters and generation-Xers who make up the majority of these 50 percent of "preventable" losses have left the church because the church has lost touch with its flock as they have wandered off. These sheep are in their productive years, bearing children and grandchildren. But the generations that in the past caused the church to flourish are today withering on the vine. Losing members to death at the end of the cycle is no crime and *is* unpreventable, but losing members in the birth and productive stage of the cycle leaves us with a shrinking circle and a declining birth rate. The inability to offset these losses, to the point of having a downward spiral, is plunging us toward spiritual and physical bankruptcy as a church. Do you find it amazing, as I do, that the population is growing, schools are crowded, cities are exploding, and the church is becoming increasingly desolate? What's wrong with this picture? I call it the ostrich syndrome!

After reviewing and compiling these statistics, I mailed them to the General Church staff person I met at that conference with a note telling him that these numbers show there are significant "preventable" losses in our church. What we need is a time of repentance for our failure in this covenant. Then we need God's blessing that we may once again regain the promises of Abraham and be ". . . like the sand of the sea, which cannot be counted" (Genesis 32:12).

My concern, and that of any pastor of the church of Jesus Christ is, "How do we change the tide?" Thus my heart and life is not focused toward hopelessness, but to Hope.[2] In 30–33 AD, Christianity grew from just a handful of followers to millions. Surely the millions of us left in the church today can turn the tide. How do we do this? This book is dedicated to this goal, and I hope to offer a fresh perspective and ways this might be done.

THE AUDIENCE

There are three ways in which church growth occurs effectively. I believe the concepts of this book, while taken from the description of a new church start, could be adapted to fit a variety of situations.

NEW SUNDAY SCHOOL AND/OR SMALL GROUPS

One possibility is through adding new Sunday school classes and/or small groups in existing churches. After 18 to 24 months, classes and small groups tend to become closed. By starting new classes and small groups on a regular basis, you make new entry points available for people to join your fellowship.

---

[2] At times I find myself capitalizing the words *Hope, Grace* and *Love.* In those cases I am using these words to personify God, and using them as proper nouns.

ADDING NEW SUNDAY WORSHIP SERVICES FOR A NEW TARGET GROUP

Another approach would be adding a new worship service to an existing congregation—a service designed to meet a specific target group. Please take care not to turn this new service into reruns of the 100-year-old traditional ten o'clock hour at the First Church Main Street USA. Baskin Robbins has been successful because they have 31 flavors—not just vanilla. Each flavor, by definition, is ice cream. Each appeals to some and is distasteful to others, but together they allow Baskin Robbins to excel in the area of ice cream sales. Similarly, churches must offer different flavors. Just because you add a seeker-sensitive service, a progressive service, a contemporary service, a drama service or a multimedia service doesn't mean you have betrayed the faith. As long as the Apostles' Creed is the basis, the Word of God is the source, Jesus Christ is the cornerstone and the Great Commission and Greatest Commandment are being proclaimed, it is still worship. Just as custard or yogurt is not ice cream, when we drop a tenant of our faith or quit proclaiming the Gospel of Grace, Love and Hope, then we have something else. But just because we try new flavors doesn't mean we have abandoned our first love. We must learn the difference.[3]

NEW CHURCH STARTS

The third way to affect church growth is by starting new churches. This can be done through three major methods: *scratch starts, satellite launching* and *hybridization.*

---

[3] I often compare the church and the various opportunities within sound Christian doctrine, meaning the Apostles' Creed, to Baskin Robbins' Ice Cream. In our faith we have many flavors: Methodist, Baptist, Presbyterian, Social Brethren, Nazarene, to name a few, each providing Christian places of worship with sound doctrine. However, the church must guard against ice cream look-alikes, such as yogurt and custard. Yogurts and custards are cults and quasi-Christian sects, like the Jehovah's Witnesses, the Mormons, and so on. These "churches" might appear to the casual observer like ice creams, but the ingredients aren't the same, and their foundations are not faithful to Christian doctrine.

SCRATCH STARTS

New planting brings the least baggage and allows for the greatest flexibility and development of an "Acts" church. This kind of church is a throwback to a time when the church was healthy, productive and adding thousands to the faith. Why? Because it was fresh, new and vibrant and the people were learning and struggling together. They didn't know all the answers, but they were holding on to the horns of the altar of Grace (see 1 Kings 1:50) to find the way.

SATELLITE LAUNCHING

The second method is by satellite launching or starting franchises. In this method, an existing church with a vibrant, growing ministry sends an effective sub-ministry team to an area that is beyond the reach of the current parish. These missionaries begin a new work with the established church's support. This method allows the new church to benefit from the existing church's experience, reputation and resourcing.

One weakness of this approach is the temptation to recreate a satellite in the sending church's own image, rather than letting it form an identity of its own. Another drawback is having a reputation that is counterproductive in a competing community and thus the new church relies on the resources of the headquarters rather than developing a solid local foundation of workers, resources and stewardship. The success of satellite churches is measured by the purposes of their leaders—whether they seek the glory of God or their own graven images.

HYBRIDIZATION

The third method is hybridization. This occurs when two small or semi-effective congregations that offer some ministry and activities but face insurmountable obstacles to growth (due to their size, location, physical plant, finances or staffing) join to form a new congregation. Together the two hybridized churches can better utilize staff, divide the cost of facilities and afford more space. If they resolve to work together, then what each brings to a new church will attract "Joe and Jane Third-Party" who would not have given either of the previously small, ineffective churches a glance. Hybridization creates a synergy where 1 + 1 = 3 (1 congregation + 1 congregation = 3, a much larger congregation).

A good model for this is the Sugar Creek United Methodist Church in the Illinois Great Rivers Conference. This church, chartered in 1995, combined a congregation of 60 with a congregation of 30. One year after their hybridization, they had grown, through synergy, to an average attendance of 200–220 in a new facility in a new site with a new name.

Hybridization works because in the past there were many small churches due to the transportation limitations of previous generations, but today's generation does not think twice about driving 15 to 20 minutes to worship. The strengths of this method are a financial base and a volume of people, equipment and experience. The weaknesses are *having* a financial base, a volume of "stuck-in-the-mud" people and too much experience to learn anything. The key to the success of this model is a dedicated, thick-hided pastor and two congregations whose desire is to build the kingdom of God instead of to preserve the "old guard of the kingdom." This model requires that the existing congregations acknowledge the reality of their situations and accept that if either of the former congregations knew everything they would not be facing this decision. This model takes courage. It requires an openness to the moving power of the Holy Spirit and an incredible willingness to be open to a God who is into new beginnings. God loves to do miracles and new things!

HERE WE GO!

The model presented in this book comes from the perspective of scratch starts, but could easily be adapted by churches interested in launching satellite churches or by multiple smaller local congregations seeking to create a hybrid church, and even by existing churches interested in creating a new worship service dedicated to a new target audience.

The Acts church began when a handful of disciples went abroad building small groups. Small groups formed churches. New churches sent out disciples to start new small groups and those small groups became churches and on and on and on . . . I am the result of the Herrin First United Methodist Church in Herrin, Illinois, being faithful in the ministry and discipleship of its members. My home church helped me to grow in grace and knowledge, and sent me out into the field to start a new small group, and to start a new church called Highland Hope. And it will be the heritage and responsibility of Highland Hope to nurture its members and send them forth to the front line where church growth continues.

One of my favorite hobbies and passions is the baking of Italian bread, and it is easy to see the parallels here. Why do I liken this process to the baking of Italian bread? Because the work of starting a church requires a passion to serve God. We need passions to motivate us to delve into things that give our hearts joy, things that allow us to relax and do great things for God.

I hope you will enjoy this book about how a church called Highland Hope was started, and that this will lead you to a vision, calling and recipe of your own for building and growing the church God has called you to serve.

GETTING STARTED: THE UTENSILS AND COOKWARE YOU NEED

DO GOOD PREP WORK

Good cooking and baking require great preparation: gathering the right ingredients, utensils, cookware and cooking surface. Nothing is more frustrating than to be making bread, hands entrenched in dough, and realize you're out of yeast or semolina flour. Now you have to stop! Good prep work will save time in the kitchen, and will make your church development more efficient and organized.

This chapter describes some of the challenges we faced in the early days of Highland Hope. As I look back, I can see how the decisions we made then shaped the direction of many other areas. Like the first domino in a series, those decisions have been literally penultimate,[1] to use a theological term meaning "not it, but close to it."

---

[1] The dictionary defines *penultimate* as "the last but one," the next to the final. It is also a theological term referring to the coming of John the Baptist as the forerunner to Jesus. These early decisions will be very influential and important to the future of the church, but in the end Christ is the bottom line.

WHAT IS NEEDED

It would be hard to tell you what is needed in your situation. Hopefully the process that I will outline will help you expose those areas that need thought and planning as you prepare your model.

While writing this book, a friend sent me an article written by an Argentinian missionary. The title of the article, selected on the other half of the globe, was "Baking a Church from Scratch." This is not where I got the title of this book, but this reveals how the One Spirit of God moves among the people. So maybe this formula will help you:

> To "bake" a church from scratch, you need a pan made out of concern, well-greased with flexibility. Stir together prayer, thoughtful preparation, patience, and several cups of smiles, hugs, and kisses. Bake as long as needed in a warm atmosphere of love, allowing the Holy Spirit to watch it closely.[2]

DO YOUR HOMEWORK

Do your homework! This is a phrase that I cannot overstate, and you will see it again and again. Whether you are making plans to target an area, planning to move in, preparing for your first contacts or starting a new program in an established congregation, doing your homework is the key. Homework includes praying, listening, planning, praying, listening, reviewing, studying, advising, pre-planning, praying, listening, sharing, expanding and acting . . . and, I promise, in all things you do prepare to be flexible. (Glad you noticed that the praying and listening

---

[2] From "Baking a Church from Scratch" by Glenda Moon. This article appeared in the January/February 1996 issue of *Call to Prayer, A Magazine of World Gospel Mission.*

kept popping up.) God will honor your planning, but God will also bless your faithfulness to the movement and leading of his Holy Spirit.

GENERAL LOCATION

General location will vary based on the project. In my situation I was appointed to Highland as the result of advanced planning done by our Annual Conference on the district level through the Conference Board of Global Ministries Committee on Parish Development. They had targeted several cities, and Highland was the number one priority on the list. I received notification of my appointment to Highland in March 1995, but I didn't have to move there until July 1995, so I had time to do my own preparation work. I could construct a budget, create a plan and develop some ownership and confidence in the location. Regardless of who picks the location, you must believe in your product and care about your market and its constituents. After the cabinet called me and informed me that I would go to Highland, the details of where, how and what were left to my development.

If you are in a situation where you are unsure of a general location, you might try the following three steps in several different prospective sites and see where God leads you. Church planting calls for lots of gut checks, so pay attention and learn to trust the rumblings and twinges in your stomach.

DO A DEMOGRAPHIC STUDY

One of the most useful and valuable tools I was given was an in-depth demographic study, called a PRISM site analysis, ordered by our Conference's Board of Global Ministries in their site planning phase. This document surveyed the Highland area and about six other nearby towns. The report broke the information down based on population, ages, incomes, education, religious affiliations, job markets and home values. It even showed the projected inflation of property values and growth of families. This information was gathered from the past 20 years and was projected into the year 2000.

As I looked at this study in comparison to the community I found it was very accurate![3] Figure 2-1 is my personal summary of the PRISM report and my own preliminary analysis.

---

[3] You can order a PRISM site analysis study by contacting the General Board of Global Ministries, Office of Research and Information Management, 475 Riverside Drive, New York, NY 10015. Phone (217) 870-3860.

FIGURE 2-1
Needs and Demographics Assessment

1. A Snap Shot:
The town of Highland, Illinois, is located in Madison County and borders St. Clair County, an area in the State of Illinois that is second in population only to the Chicago area. The town is only 25 miles east of downtown St. Louis, Missouri, and is accessed by taking exit #23 off Interstate 70. As a small town resting in the shadows of the famous St. Louis Arch, Highland has become a bedroom community to both the St. Louis and metro east areas.

2. History of Methodism in Highland:
The Methodist church has not served the Highland community for over 100 years. The original Methodist Church in Highland was founded in 1846. It was a cooperative church, housing both a German Methodist congregation and an American Methodist congregation. But it was not long before the church fell into dissension between the English- and German-speaking Methodists. The church was closed around the turn of the century. Over the next 100 years, Highland continued to be a fairly sequestered Swiss-German settlement.

3. A Sociological Look at Highland:
Highland is a growing community of approximately 13,000 residents within the 62249 Zip Code. The city of Highland has risen to the occasion by building a new sportsplex, is in the process of making a substantial addition to the high school and is making preparations for a new junior high school in the future. Highland is home to one of the finest county fairgrounds and town squares in the southern Illinois area. Highland has changed significantly over the last 15 years, from a farming and industrial community to a white-collar community. It has become a commuter bedroom community to the greater metropolitan region with over 53% of the work force earning their incomes from white-collar jobs. Over 45% of the residents commute 20–60 minutes to work, and over 54% of the residents have lived in Highland 10 years or less with over 40% of the population having located to Highland in the last five years. What a Boom! What an opportunity! Less than 13% of the population is over the age of 65, with 37% falling between the ages of 25 and 49, and another 14% between ages 50 and 64. With the nearest higher learning institutions 20 miles away, Highland only boasts about 8% of its population between 18 and 25. The high concentration of adults in their child-bearing years has resulted in 27% of the population being under age 17.

4. An Economical Picture of Highland:

Prior to 1980, Highland was a relatively closed Swiss-German settlement with a population of approximately 6,000 residing in a town of some 2,000 residences. As the St. Louis and metro east areas have filled to capacity, Highland has been affected by their overflowing growth. In a little over 14 years, the community has blossomed to 13,000 residents living in some 4,500 residences. As we write this profile, an additional 500 homes are in some phase of development and are targeted for completion in the next two years. Property values have skyrocketed with the average acre of land going from a 1980 value of $2,500 to a current $10,000 per acre cost. Home values have increased from a 1980 value of $62,000 to a current $115,000+ value, with a projected increase of another 16% by 1999. Household income has kept pace as the average household income has gone from a 1980 value of $20,000 to a current $39,000 with 15% growth projected over the next five years. In years past, the primary job market was farming and manufacturing, but the latest boom has transformed some of that farm land into subdivisions, with development continuing to expand.

5. The Ecumenical Community of Highland:

The blossoming town of Highland has a great demand for a United Methodist Church. Highland is presently home to one Roman Catholic Church, an Evangelical Reformed United Church of Christ, a Congregational Church, a Missouri Synod Lutheran Church, one small Southern Baptist Church, a small American Baptist congregation, and an 18-year-old nondenominational community church. At present, the dominant churches of the community are the Roman Catholic and United Church of Christ. These are the only churches with average attendance above 250, and they clearly represent the pre-1980 Swiss-German flavor of the community. When asked about the predominant religious influence on the community the average Highlander responds, "This is a Catholic town." However, it is also the headquarters of the Illinois South Conference of the United Church of Christ, and as such the Evangelical United Church of Christ represents the second largest religious sector. As the town has grown, the new residents coming to Highland bring a "Christian Protestant" background approximately 80% of the time. Some figures estimate that 70% of the Highland residents are not active in a local church. We believe there is a need for a church here and that this growth curve represents our niche.

Information in this analysis is condensed from a PRISM site analysis study. These studies are available by contacting the General Board of Global Ministries, Office of Research and Information Management, 475 Riverside Drive, New York, NY 10015. Phone (217) 870-3860.

DEFINE YOUR TARGET MARKET AND AUDIENCE

I know it is early. I know you're thinking, "I haven't even begun the church yet." I know your mother taught you not to stereotype people, but there is a biblical mandate for taking some time and making some preliminary decisions (See Luke 14:28, 31). Because your funding, budgeting and initial strategies for the future will depend on your vision now, don't be too nearsighted.

> **S**uppose one of you wants to build a tower. Will he not first sit down and estimate the cost to see if he has enough money to complete it? ... Or suppose a king is about to go to war against another king. Will he not first sit down and consider whether he is able with ten thousand men to oppose the one coming against him with twenty thousand? (Luke 14:28, 31)

This does not mean you cannot adjust or expand your plans later; it just means a well-thought-out and prayed-out initial plan of attack is essential. If you are gifted in the area of church planting, which the Bible defines in Ephesians as being an apostle or a planter of churches, then God's Holy Spirit will lead you in this process.

This concept guided me through the early budget planning. Though it had to be revised several times, this concept told me where to look for a home and what resources we would need to meet the demands of the target group. Remember—in today's world, if you try to be everything to everyone you will not be able to start that church on limited funds. Take a risk; pick the target group with the highest percentage likelihood of success. The key to Highland Hope's being a successful new church in the Highland community was choosing programs and targeting a demographic group of people that no other church was currently reaching.

As you plan to reach your target group, keep this advice in mind: ***Create your own niche, but watch out for nooks—we have enough of them.*** A nook is a clique. One dictionary defines a clique as "an exclusive social group." It can also be a small group of insiders that repel new persons and ideas. On the other hand, a niche, according to the same dictionary, is "a semi-enclosed place." It is a unique spot, but still accessible for those who wish to come and go.

Figure 2-2 describes the "target family" Highland Hope aimed to reach. Your target family could be affluent retirees, struggling single-parent households, or any other unserved demographic group in your community.

SELECT A WORKING AREA

Pick a place to prepare your bread that will be effective and useful. You don't want to start making bread and find that you're too far from the outlet needed to run the mixer, or so far from the sink that you will waste lots of steps. The same goes for church planting.

Where will you live? Where will your office be? Where can your small groups meet? What about nursery care during those meetings?

FIGURE 2-2
The Target Family of Highland Hope

The target family is a two-income family in their 20s to late 40s having two to three children 0–17 years of age. The family most likely has moved to this area in the last five years, and has not found a church home in the fairly steadfast Swiss-German dominated churches. The family is probably not "denominationally conscious," but would identify themselves as Protestants. However, their parents were probably associated with a church in their childhood. This family probably lives in a subdivision on the outskirts of town and is probably struggling on the career ladder to support their $100,000+ mortgage and the two cars (mostly likely a sedan and a mini-van). This target audience may be church friendly but as typical baby boomers, busters and Xers they have probably not been active in church since their childhoods. To develop a congregation we will focus on creating a sense of belonging, with a special emphasis on the unique opportunity for families to shape their own quality adult, youth and children's ministries programs designed to fit the needs of the family of the 1990s.

Where in the community can you rent or borrow "neutral space" for your church to meet? All these questions have to be answered. It doesn't mean you can't move, or combine them through multiuse facilities, but the key is that careful thought is given to each of these areas. They will shape your ministry immensely.

WHERE TO LIVE?

Most likely you will not be moving to a church-owned parsonage, unless your funding allows you to purchase one. You are probably on a meager salary. However, the community you're moving to is likely a high growth, high property value, high everything community—if it is not, it may not be the growing community needed to start a fast-growing church. Given the realities of this situation, you have to use your limited funds with maximum impact.

I chose a subdivision a half mile outside the city limits. Most of the growth in our area is occurring within a three-mile radius of the city limits. I chose a house that was accessible and easy to give directions to. It was a new home on a corner lot of two acres, which has allowed room for all kinds of activities and youth functions. (I even had our church sponsored tee-ball practices here.) In addition, I really looked at how much parking I could handle. Figuring that a home fellowship group or ministry team could have up to 30 participants, what would I do with 10 to 15 cars on my street? Would my neighbors be upset? Would I block driveways? In this subdivision the homes were on two-acre county lots, instead of one-third-acre town lots, and I had plenty of room. Given my two-acre lot, I was able to put in a parking area that could handle at least 10 cars, and I still have room for another 10 on the street without creating neighborhood chaos.

What kind of home? I picked a typical home in the community with 1,350 square feet (three bedrooms, a living room, kitchen, two baths, a two-car oversized garage and an unfinished basement of another 1350 square feet). I had to make another very important decision—whether to rent or own the home. Figure 2-3 is the pro and con list I used to make this decision. As you can see, the pro and con side of the decision to rent was extensive and balanced, and certainly not exhaustive, but the pro side of buying outweighed its con. Of course, if the resources aren't there, the con aspect of buying is clearly a major factor.

My personal feeling is that by purchasing a home you make a statement of permanency. There are very few things I would insist on from

Getting Started: The Utensils and Cookware You Need 29

FIGURE 2-3
The Rent vs. Purchase Decision

Rent	Purchase
Pro	*Pro*
1. Less capital needed	1. Statement of permanence
2. Flexibility (one-year lease)	2. Investment in the community
3. No unforeseen maintenance costs/more budgetable	3. YOURS—Can decorate and adapt
4. Ready made/not labor intensive	4. Personal investment/equity
5. Not yours	5. Can become church owned/transferable
6. No property taxes	6. Not church owned—an oasis!
Con	*Con*
1. Often limited parking	1. Down-payment, cost, taxes and maintenance (not tax-exempt until church owned)
2. Space cannot be changed without approval	2. Wear and tear on your home
3. Rent is expended without long-term return	
4. How many in your congregation rent? Most high growth communities are residential	
5. May or may not be bought for a permanent parsonage	

---

my district superintendent, but one is that enough conference funding is budgeted for a housing allowance that provides for the purchase of something in a neighborhood that holds people of your target group. Your neighbors will provide you with the best PR—word of mouth. They will lead you to people who will most likely become active participants in your new church.

By purchasing a home, you will be able to do more with the property, and are less likely to be sabotaged by the idle chatter of a landlord prereleasing his opinion of you and your job. For the first two months after I moved into my house, no one knew who, what or why I was there, unless I chose to tell them. This allowed me to set the tone and not become the subject of the local grapevine's gossip.

WHERE WILL YOUR OFFICE BE?

You will need an office, a business address and, most importantly, you will need a church phone. Don't forget to plan ahead, because your next phone book listing is one of your most important ventures. You will be setting the tone for all those residents and especially newcomers to the town who are looking for a church home over the next year.

Figure 2-4 is the 1996–1997 Highland phone directory ad. This ad was ordered in November of 1995 and was accurate, but was planned one month before our first service and seven months before the directory came out in the summer of 1996. When I planned this Yellow Pages ad, little of this was a certainty, but I would rather be slightly off than not on at all. This is a good example of why you need to do your homework when starting a new church from scratch.

FIGURE 2-4
Highland Hope 1996–1997 Telephone Directory Ad

Highland Hope United Methodist Church

**Sunday School 9:30 AM & Worship at 10:30 AM in the
Highland Middle School Auditorium at the
Corner of Poplar & Lindenthal Ave.**
*Nursery Care Provided – Children's Church
Youth Activities – Accessibility – Home Fellowships*

Rev. Troy D. Benitone, Pastor
Church Ofc.: 23 Triland Ct., Highland 654-8434

We purchased a home with enough living space for our family and ample parking space for holding small group fellowships and activities in our home. Since I was given NO budget for an office anywhere else, I decided to risk $6,000 of my personal savings (which was later reimbursed by an unexpected and appreciated extended grant from our Annual Conference) to put the church office in my basement. With this $6,000 I purchased all the supplies to finish the basement and expand the driveway. (In the county, gravel and railroad ties were in fashion, while the city required asphalt or concrete, which would be very expensive. Another plus to living outside town is relaxed building and zoning codes.)

A friend of mine from Olney drew up the basement blueprints. Rev. Shane Bishop's churches in Sumner, Illinois, after learning about the need during a men's breakfast, committed to doing the carpentry work, and another pastoral colleague provided parishioners with expertise at putting up suspended ceilings. Others laid carpet, and, finally, from my home church I sought out a plumber and my grandfather to do the plumbing and finishing work. I hired the heating and air conditioning contractors; so as not to void my warranty, I had them add four ducts and a return in the basement for a total of $150. I also contracted to have the sheetrock taped, textured and painted for $700. All of the work was done and supervised by professional carpenters or craftsmen. It was essential that the work be excellent to fit the value of this $105,000 home. My post-construction remodeling appraisal was $129,000, thanks to their excellent work.

The basement contained a restroom, pastor's study, a copier workroom and a meeting area large enough for 30 persons. We also designed a small playroom. Six months later, we walled out another area to add an office for my new administrative assistant, Connie Pellock, and added extensive shelving to the playroom and garage.

You might ask, "What is it like to have an office in the house?" Well, it is convenient and accessible. I know, based on the work level and requirements of starting a church, that had my office been elsewhere I would never have seen my lovely wife and beautiful children. I can get up and help with something or stop to talk with them, or at least be there for them to talk at me, versus not being there at all or having to waste time making a commute. (However, to hear my wife's side of the story, see Figure 2-5!) As for the telephone, we have separate personal and church phone lines and a nice intercom system with an answering machine. Still, the phone drives us nuts at times. You would be surprised at who will call a church office and at what time.

FIGURE 2-5
My Wife's Point of View on the Church Office

Have you ever heard an older woman telling about how upsetting it is to have her retired husband hanging around the house and getting in the way? Well, I can relate. However, instead of my husband sitting around doing nothing, I found that his busyness was spilling over into my life and, quite frankly, interrupting my routine. Prior to our marriage, one of the agreements we made was that I would not work outside the home. Rather, I would stay at home with our kids and be a housewife. I know the thought of being a housewife isn't very pleasant for some women, but I was made for the job. I love being able to play with my kids, read them books, watch Sesame Street and Barney and fit in a little housework here and there. Well, somehow, when we moved to Highland my job title changed. Not only was I the pastor's wife, I also became the church secretary, janitor, hostess, receptionist, etc. (I am sooo thankful for Connie [the administrative assistant].)

We moved to Highland and into this position with our eyes wide open, but you really can't understand the amount of work required to start a church until you get into it. The first year was the busiest yet the most fulfilling year of our married life. We both felt called to start this church, and having the office in our home gave me a unique opportunity to meet every individual who was involved with our church. What a blessing!

Whether or not to have the church office in your home should be thought out carefully. If you and your spouse (and kids) don't agree fully, it will be very difficult. You have to realize that not only will every adult pass through your house, but so will their kids. Thankfully, most of the people in our church are very respectful of our home, but you're always going to have a small percentage of people who aren't so thoughtful. You should set up definite boundaries right from the start. Let people know what parts of your house are considered open and what parts are not. Respect your kids' territory. Don't let everyone else's kids play in their rooms. Our kids have been really good sports about this whole thing, and they actually seem to enjoy it. Just use wisdom and try to stay positive.

> One definite plus about having Troy here is that I can leave the kids with him anytime I need to. Also, it's nice to be able to see him anytime, and I know the kids appreciate that, too.
>
> I have to admit, sometimes I long for the days when Troy would leave the house in the morning and return that evening. But, overall, this has been a great experience, and I wouldn't trade it for anything.
>
> Beth Benitone

After we moved into our new home, a trickle of people began stopping by the office, mostly area pastors, conference officials and friends. But within three months as many as 30 people were coming to our home two nights a week for Bible study, early youth group meetings of eight to ten kids, leadership team meetings and so forth. Every night, every day, at 8 A.M., 10 A.M., 1 P.M., 6 P.M., 8 P.M., 11 P.M. or *anytime,* there might be people meeting with or without me in our home/office. As most of our ministries are not led by me, I simply made everyone feel that our basement was the church office and they were free to meet in it. Most of the time we were blessed to see our house bustling with the faces and voices of excited people, dreaming and working together to build a great community of faith. But even Jesus, at times, had to go apart. I quickly learned that to take time out meant we had to leave our home and go out.

Given our growth and needs right now, and the fact that we have charted and are a healthy and growing congregation, we could consider moving our office to another site, but still my family time would be limited. This would also defer resources aimed at ministry, which would effect our saving of funds aimed toward a permanent land and building site. So as of today (January 23, 1997) all of our day-to-day functions still run out of our basement. We still hold most team meetings, youth group functions and other activities in our home with the exception of the music ministry, which meets at the home of our gracious Hope Ensemble leader, and our women's ministries, which move from house to house and/or frequent the home of our women's ministry coordinator. I do not regret our choice, and I would do it again on a future church start, but it is certainly a point for deep consideration and prayer. It is a little like having an open house every day. If you have an introverted personality, this would probably be a bad choice for you. (Of course, if you are that type of person, you may want to reconsider the decision to start a new church altogether.) The call is yours!

WHERE WILL WE MEET TO WORSHIP?

At this point, you have no church membership and no building; your "church" is simply a pastor, a pastor's family, a home and a lot of work ahead. But in order to be prepared and know what kind of options are available, you need to survey possible Sunday morning meeting locations. Some of the options we looked at included park facilities, community buildings, area social clubs, other churches and even the local theater. Finally we chose to meet in the middle school auditorium.

We seriously considered the park facility, where we could utilize the county fair exposition building, but we would not have been able to get a long-term continuous lease, and could only get approximately 35 to 40 Sundays guaranteed. Thus we would be faced with finding alternative locations on at least 12 to 17 Sundays. How do you plan, promote and advertise for a location that is temporary? We looked at organizations such as the VFW, the American Legion and the Masonic lodge. Each would have taken us, but my decision was that being new, first impressions were everything, and I did not want the new church to be saddled with the baggage, community history or politics of any of these organizations. I am aware of a couple of successful churches that have started in buildings such as these, when all else failed.

Our final decision was to enter into a long-term lease of the Highland Middle School Auditorium. This location gave us the use of a neutral location with adequate parking, great facilities (including handicap accessibility), an auditorium with seating and plenty of classrooms, not to mention custodial service. I do have an emergency alternative plan to use our local theater in the event of a school schedule conflict, a utility systems failure or other such crisis. The cost of our facility is $50 per week plus the required wages of a Sunday janitor from the school during the four hours we use the building. This runs about $20 per hour—double overtime, per their contract. So our cost is approximately $130–$150 per week. Pretty reasonable!

Every situation will differ, but our relationship with the school system has been great. Our congregation includes about a dozen members who work in the local schools, including the principal of the building in which we meet. We have been real partners with the school, never overstepping our appropriate bounds, and even loaning our sound system to the school system on many occasions. Our sound system is top rate and totally portable, and we always provide an operator. We never ask for anything in return, but they always recognize our church and the operator in these events. These school audiences are the age of our target group, so this is another win-win opportunity. We have become, I believe, real friends and supporters of the Highland school system. We try to give back!

WRITING A VISION, MISSION AND PHILOSOPHY STATEMENT

I know it's early in the church planting process and you haven't even met the future members of your congregation. By crafting your vision, mission and philosophy statement now, you're not letting them help shape your identity. But did the Apostle Paul walk into a town and stop to take a straw poll on how he should go about doing the Great Commission? No! Of course, after a home church had begun and leaders were selected Paul placed the Great Commission in their laps and left for new territory. There is no law against having your developing church redesign, refine and redraw these statements as often as needed or necessary. But you are the pastor assigned to plant the church, and the first vision, mission and philosophy statements must rest in your gifts and abilities. If your vision is for a church with an effective children's ministry, you'd better like that kind of ministry. It will show if you don't.

Over our first year and in our pastor's classes we updated our mission statement several times to correct the tenses from future tense to present tense, but in general the statement has remained true to the original vision. Figure 2-6 shows our vision statement as it reads today.

THE COOKWARE: YOUR ACCOUNTABILITY TEAM AND FAMILY SUPPORT

One of the essentials in any program is cookware. If you want good bread, careful selection of cookware is essential. I always bake my Italian bread on terra-cotta tiles, which makes my crust hard and thick. This is the real secret to great Italian bread. In the same way, your family, your friends and your mentors will play an important role in baking a great church.

I remember the call and my excitement when the district superintendent informed me of my appointment by then-Bishop David Lawson to

FIGURE 2-6
The Vision Statement of Highland Hope

Highland Hope is:

A New Developing Congregation.
A Place to Grow Spiritually.
An Opportunity for Involvement in a
New Christian Fellowship.

Highland Hope is for:

People Looking for a Church Home.
People Who Want a Church That Is Exciting and Fun.
People of All Ages and Stages.

Highland Hope is in Need of:

People Who Want to Be a Part of Something New.
People Who Want to Create a Church to Meet Today's Needs.
People Who Want to Love God With All Their Hearts,
Minds, Souls and Strength.

The Vision:

Highland Hope is a vision—a vision of a new church congregation designed to meet the spiritual needs of the Highland family. Highland Hope is for people with hopes and dreams, people who want to better learn to love God and each other. Highland Hope is about people. One of our key hopes is that people will get to know one another, develop relationships and build trust. These will be the key factors in developing a strong foundation to the church. After all, a church is about people and not buildings. If the people of Highland Hope are strong, the church will be strong.

The Mission:

Our mission is to be a part of the Highland community, to grow in faith and to share Christ. We are here to provide this kind of HOPE: "But in your hearts set apart Christ as Lord. Always be prepared to give an answer to everyone who asks you to give the reason for the hope that is within you" (1 Peter 3:15).

the Highland community to plant a new church. I jumped for joy. My wife Beth and I went out on what we called "celebration meals" for a week. Our dreams and hopes were becoming a reality. What a sense of excitement this created in our lives, to be the pastor of a new, vibrant and explosive congregation. I had no doubt that God would do great things.

We loaded up the truck on June 29 and moved into our home on June 30. We had gone through this process before in our previous moves to the churches in Georgia and Illinois. We had always enjoyed the honeymoon experience of our first days at each of these churches. Everyone was friendly, parishioners would offer to take us out to Sunday lunch and the ladies of the church would drop meals by that entire first week. When we moved to Georgia we found the parsonage pantry, refrigerator and breadbox full of groceries. People were even there to help with the unloading—people, people, people.

As we pulled into Highland late on the evening of June 30 we crawled into the house, carrying our sleeping children, Heather (12), Joshua (4) and Caleb (2), placing them on the two mattresses that we had moved over a week earlier. Beth and I grabbed the other mattress out of the truck, drug it into our room, threw it on our floor and crashed for the night. It is amazing how quickly morning comes in a house without window treatments. We awoke the next morning bright and early to an empty house, an empty refrigerator and an empty pantry. Our coffee maker was stuck in the back of the 26-foot U-haul. We sat down on the floor. We looked at each other for a while. There wasn't even a clock in the house.

Finally, we went to town to get coffee and breakfast. But there no one greeted us. There was no, "Hi, Rev. Troy!" We went home. I looked at the truck, and it was still full! The kitchen was still barren. I checked the answering machine, which had been hooked up for a week, but no one had left a single message. This went on for a week. Two weeks. Would you believe three? How about four! Would you believe it? NO ONE knew we were there. What a feeling! No welcome wagon, no pastor's family potluck, no big first Sunday greeting, no one, nothing, zip! The mountain was before us and, despite my super-extroverted-type-A personality which very rarely sags, I was depressed. We were alone! I felt like Charlie Brown. If you don't understand personality types, let me explain. Solitude will drive type A-extroverts crazy. But I will tell you as I write this one year later, I would like a few weeks of that crazy time back. I think I could handle it now.

That's why family, friends and mentors are essential. They are your source of encouragement, your sounding board, your cheerleaders. They are it! My family, from day one, has been a missionary family completely and unselfishly devoted to planting this church in Highland. They have shared their home with what seems like every single person in Highland. Every child has played with every one of our kids' toys, and a few toys have even been broken, without a single complaint from my kids (they have very kind and generous hearts). My wife has made somewhere in the neighborhood of 400,000 pots of coffee,[4] cleaned the house in preparation for a literal open house everyday, for what is now over 1,000 days, and licked, stuffed, stamped and prepared mailings galore.[5] It goes on and on. If it were not for my family, for my friends who called and said, "How are you doing?" at crucial times, for the mentor church pastors keeping their relationships with me and the support of the Highland Launch Team, I believe I would have gone stark raving mad.

One of the programs I created to develop a family of support for me professionally, especially in the area of prayer and emergency support, was the Mentor Church Program. *(See the Appendix for a complete description of this program.)* Four churches were asked to represent a God-family, like Godparents, to enter into a covenant to assist the pastor and church at Highland in their spiritual growth. These four churches were asked to fill certain roles. Each church was asked because of a particular area of ministry in which they would be able to give us witness, direction and training, and that would be very important to our development.

Our God-family had a good genetic makeup. Each of these churches was one of the top 10 of our conference, with St. Matthew being first, O'Fallon second, Aldersgate third and Sumner-Beulah ninth. The father church was St. Matthew UMC, which was the largest church in the former Southern Illinois Conference. They had grown from a mere handful of 50 people in the 1960s to an average attendance of over 1,300 today. Their music, their facility, their staffing and their evangelistic outreach were and are witnesses to us of what God could do with Highland Hope in a short time.

Our mother church was the Aldersgate UMC in Marion, Illinois, where Rev. James Slone is the pastor. Jim's preaching is consistently challenging and deeply thought-provoking. Also, Aldersgate has one of the strongest intercessory prayer ministries around.

---

[4] Note to literalists: This is an exaggeration.

[5] The "1,000 days of open house" and "mailings galore" are understatements to balance the coffee comment. Oh, yes, when you make coffee, you have to have a pot of decaffeinated, too.

The other two were sibling churches. The O'Fallon UMC was our brother church in O'Fallon, Illinois. This is a church near our community that reaches out to a vast number of people much like our own demographic makeup. Thus, they were a fast-growing church. The strength that Rev. Dwight Jones, the pastor, brought to our God-family was that he had served as a former district superintendent, and now as the pastor of our conference's second largest and still fast growing congregation. Dwight understands administration, the people, the pulpit and the problems pastors, conference leaders and the church are facing. He was like a big brother to me so many times, giving advice and support on numerous occasions, not to mention loaning us the keys to their van several times. That's what big brothers do! "Thanks, Bro!"

The last church, our sister church, was actually a charge composed of two churches, the Sumner UMC and the Beulah UMC, served by Rev. Shane Bishop. Shane was our conference's 1996 Harry Denman Evangelism Award winner. This award is given to only one of our conference's clergy each year for outstanding work in the area of evangelism and church growth. Shane's churches had added over 100 members in the last three years, and the charge was the ninth largest charge in our conference,[6] despite being located in a town of just 1,100 people. What is amazing about the Sumner-Beulah United Methodist charge is that all of the other top 10 charges are situated in large population centers of 20,000 or better. We certainly could learn from this church and its vision. This church has been there for us so many times. They were the church that came over and did a large part of the work on our basement. They have blessed us with generous financial gifts to assist us in purchasing our land sooner. Not to mention, their pastor, and closest friend, served as my counselor, advisor, friend, lunch buddy, crying towel and everything else during those first months, and even until this day.

Pastors, to be successful, I encourage and implore you to find one or two colleagues you can trust who will hold your confidence. I have enclosed in the Appendix a copy of the Highland Hope Mentor Program that I wrote for my church start. I invite you to use it if it fits your needs. Each of these churches have stayed, prayed and been there for us from day one to this day. As we Italians say, "Family is family, and family takes care of family, and there is no one better to take care of you than family."

---

[6] These figures are based on the former Southern Illinois Conference and not the newly merged Illinois Great Rivers Conference for which these rankings would be different. There were approximately 395 churches in the former conference and over 1,011 in the new conference.

THE UTENSILS: CONNECTIONAL SUPPORT AND FUNDING

It is essential to good church development to get your house in order and create a good base of support. I spent two months preaching at church camps that first summer, preaching revivals, going to men's and/or women's breakfasts, and wherever I could to share about the project at Highland Hope. From day one until the charter of Highland Hope (July 1, 1995–October 20, 1996), I wrote a column entitled "Highland Hope" for our conference's monthly newspaper. I believe this helped keep area Methodists informed on our process, inviting them to participate in special projects and asking them to keep us in their prayers. This has been a central key to our connectional support from the 395 churches (the number of churches in the former Southern Illinois Conference) who have supported and prayed for our welfare and success. In the first year alone these churches gave our local church about $20,000, which made the purchase of our 15-acre site a reality much sooner. As of January 1998, over 126 of these churches have provided on-site labor, financial support or prayer covering for our project. Maintain relationships!

HANDLING THE BUCKS

Let me state this up front. Do not attempt to be the pastor and the treasurer simultaneously. It is not good procedure nor is it prudent. By creating countermeasures up front, you will develop a good advisor who will be knowledgeable about the life of the church from a fiduciary standpoint.

When the Highland Hope project was initiated, and I was appointed to the Highland parish, I had no oversight or advisory committee within a church to work with, to give me counsel, to support me and my family in crisis or to be my advocate in times of personal need. So my district superintendent at that time proposed the designation of a Highland Launch Team to work with me in a pastoral advisory process. Ultimately the task was mine, but their counsel and direction were there to help, support and protect me.

I helped choose the personnel and recommended the chair, who was the pastor of the largest neighboring United Methodist Church. Normally many would think this unwise, but Rev. Dennis Price, by action, deed and word believes in church growth. I believe that by choosing him, my closest United Methodist competitor, and by learning to get along and work with him, our church, as a denomination, gained better name recognition in our area. Dennis is one of those rare pastors who understands God's vision for the church. He has never seen our church or any other church as competition, but he sees the church as united in fulfilling the same commission.

I also chose a lay person and longtime family friend with a career in church finance to be my treasurer and the one responsible for the conference funds via a voucher system until charter, when the local church would assume the oversight of its funding. I owe a tremendous thanks to Keith Hindman for his friendship, faithfulness, counsel and wisdom in caring for the financial affairs of the church start.

We also had help from a local person named Carolyn Winkler, who was a member in Dennis's Church at Troy and a Highland resident. Carolyn became the local church's treasurer, and her family has become very dear to us, as her husband Mark serves as our lay leader, and our kids are interchangeable. All I can say is the rest is Greek to me. Between Keith and Carolyn, they have managed all of the finances with incredible grace, wisdom and a love for the church of Jesus Christ.

I have made a choice to not be informed as to the personal giving of members of Highland Hope. I know there are lots of different philosophies about this, but I don't want such knowledge to effect my ministry. Also, I don't want people to ever feel odd about talking with me. So the only time I ask for personal giving information is once a year when we are choosing leadership team members. I simply ask Carolyn, "Is [NAME] giving to the church, and if so, is it in a manner you feel that is appropriate? Thumbs up or thumbs down?"

Establish your financial policy early, be up front about it and be consistent.

BUDGETING/FUNDING

In the United Methodist system, church starts are funded through the connectional giving of all the churches in our annual conference through the Board of Global Ministries. The process outlined in this book assumes an outside start-up funding source that will provide salary, office, worship and setup expenses for the first year, with the new church being weaned from this funding as it develops. If you do not have similar resources or the support of some sponsoring organization or churches, then my prayers are with you, and you will have difficulty following my recipe. In my case I received a five-year funding plan with the first two years at full funding, and a planned drop-back of 33% in each of the years three, four and five. I have included in the Appendix a copy of our first year's budget and conference funding designed by me, and a copy of year two, set by the local church. Year two will reflect the addition of local church dollars, added staff and the new ministries as developed by our local congregation. See the Appendix for a sample copy of the 1996 conference budget and the 1997 first local budget. Also included is a list of setup items needed.

ALL THOSE NUMBERS AND TAX STUFF

Another important task is to get a Federal Employer Identification Number (a FEIN), which will be needed for payroll, to establish checking accounts, etc. The next task will be to establish tax exemption. In the state of Illinois, and in many states, churches can receive a tax exempt number to avoid having to pay sales tax on purchases. This number is used often in ordering supplies, purchasing equipment and building materials. You will need to establish and file with the IRS the forms needed to become a 501(c)3 exempt religious affiliated organization. Why? So that your financial contributors can receive tax credit for their charitable gifts.

As a United Methodist Church, Highland Hope falls under our conference's tax-exempt number, though you can file for your own. We also fall under the denomination's 501(c)3 status, as we are not a local church, but one local congregation, and all gifts received locally are given to the whole church with local agency over those funds. And don't forget to apply for your U.S. Postal bulk mailing permit—you will need it, and it will take a few weeks to obtain. The Appendix contains a sample SS-4 application for the FEIN, a sample Illinois Sales Tax Exemption letter and an IRS letter showing the 501(c)3 status.

CABINETS, DRAWERS AND PANTRIES: CHECK YOUR RESOURCES

Nothing drives a cook crazier than having to cook in a strange kitchen. Where is the colander? Where is the ground pepper? Where are the mixing bowls? Where is . . . ? When I enter a strange kitchen my first move is to check out the pantry, open all the drawers and peek in all the cabinets. When you move into the community where you're going to start a church, use your first month or two as top-secret, CIA, FBI, joint-investigation covert operation spy time. You are a spy charged with the mission of checking out everything. You will never be able to walk around unnoticed again, especially in a small community, because after your picture is plastered in the paper and your face is on a brochure sitting in everyone's house—trust me, it will never be the same.

VISIT CITY COMMAND AND CONTROL CENTERS

To continue our analogy to a covert operation, they speak of "command and control centers" in the military. Identify all of these in your community. Be sure to note the formal and informal structures. If you have pastored before, you will have observed that all churches have both formal and informal chains of command. The same is true for a town or city. Here is a list of a few places and things you should get familiar with during your top-secret investigation. The things you learn will be essential in reviewing and adjusting your vision, mission and philosophy statement to fit your community, before your PR campaign begins.

FORMAL COMMAND AND CONTROL CENTERS

1. ***City Council, Mayor's Office, City Manager.*** Visit a couple of council meetings as a spectator. Walk through the offices, notice wall hangings, desks and decor. Remember, these are the city leaders. They will reflect local trends.
2. ***Schools and School Board.*** Take a tour of the schools. The kindergarten will tell you a lot. The junior high will give you a window to see what trouble spots are starting to grow—this is the incubator for future community problems. Visit the high school. What kind of clubs, activities and sports are available? What are the kids wearing? Visit a school board meeting or two. I visit a school board and city council meeting at least every other month. It's been very helpful.
3. ***Chamber of Commerce.*** Ask for some information on the community. They have information on more than just local businesses.

4. ***Hospitals.*** Visit the local medical facilities. Do they have a chapel and/or a pastoral care services department?
5. ***Churches.*** Drive past all of the churches. Don't blab. Remember, you're a spy. Stop in if you dare, but be discreet. Do not lie, just be careful. You do not want another church to start your PR campaign for you. Look at the decor, scout out their sanctuary, peek at the average attendance versus membership. Is this church growing, static or dying? *Static churches are dying churches,* because when sheep are being lost in the world the church is smaller. Don't visit the pastors now—we will come back to that later in this book.
6. ***Parks and recreation areas.*** Visit all the parks and recreation areas to see what the community does. What kind of festivals and events are popular in the city? My Swiss-German town has several major festivals each year that provide good booth opportunities, not for sales, but for PR by selling something. We sold blooming onions in our first six months and were the highest grossing booth for the Jaycees, the festival sponsor. Our picture was even in the paper. What a plug! Not to mention 30 of our people, all new, got to work together for two days. I would have lost money for this experience, and had planned to! This festival booth gave me a glimpse at our developing leadership and how they work together. They did great.

INFORMAL COMMAND AND CONTROL CENTERS

These are the best indicators of a community's nature, as these people are not paid to be nice and flowery as in the formal centers.

1. ***Visit with your real estate agent.*** Where is the community growing? How is the city handling it? Do the city fathers hate the growth? This is important to know! How will they respond to a new, growing church? Based on my local information, I adjusted our PR campaign to alleviate some of those fears. I connected our church start to our ancestor, the German Methodist church, that had shut its doors in Highland about the 1920s. Everyone knew where the Old Methodist Hill was, and many of the older folks remembered that the combination of the cholera epidemic around the turn of the century and World War I forced the church to close and give its building to the Woodmen of the World. Because the Methodists still had a reputation of grace amongst the older generation of our community, we were viewed as family returning home. Perception is everything! Do your homework.

2. ***Postal carrier.*** Chat with him or her.
3. ***Coffee shops and restaurants.*** Visit the eating places and coffee houses, and sit quietly each morning. Read the local paper in-depth for a month, then keep reading it. And listen—don't talk, you will just get yourself in trouble. "Remember 007, discretion is the key!" In these places the news will be raw and unadulterated. Most will be distorted, possibly exaggerated and some will be plain old gossip, but the truth, unfortunately, is not always the reality. Perception of the truth is reality, believe it or not. At least you will learn how people perceive, translate and transform information.
4. ***Barber shops/beauty shops.*** Get your hair cut, get the kids' hair cut, your spouse's, your dogs' if there is a vet. Try different places. Ask them about the community. These people love to talk; it's half of their job. Didn't you watch the *Andy Griffith Show*?
5. ***Police officers and fire fighters.*** Ask if there is anything special you need to be aware of. Remember, the child molester law allows police to tell you about dangers right in your own neighborhood. Ask about the typical crimes or fires. Ask whether either department has a chaplaincy program. (I know you're divulging information by asking this question!) If they don't, come back in a few weeks and offer to be the police and/or fire chaplain, but don't offer now or they'll think you're wacko. To be a fire or police chaplain often entitles an informal or formal relationship with the department where you will come out to situations and fires to assist with needs, carry water, get coffee, pray with families, arrange for lodging. etc. You might even be called if they have someone contemplating suicide. Find a niche in the community.
6. ***Sporting events.*** Go to football games, T-ball games, girls' softball games, etc. Watch the parents at these T-ball or softball games. Do the parents think this is the world series, or are they laid back? In my community, nonvarsity sports are not very competitive, and the atmosphere is low pressure.

GET THE LAY OF THE LAND

The best thing I did was to map the community. Over the course of a few afternoons I loaded my wife and kids in the van, broke the city into four quadrants and drove every street, dead-end path and gravel road in a three-mile radius, in and outside of the town. In order to have an updated and accurate map, we created our own map on paper as we drove. Now, believe me, we got some strange looks as we drove slowly through the streets. People probably thought we were casing them out or maybe looking to steal a kid or something. In an effort to pacify our children, who were stuck in the van with us for hours, we told them to pretend that we were the crew of the Starship Enterprise beaming down to a planet to seek out new life forms, with "the prime-directive" not to interfere or let them know about us. This helped our kids tolerate this tedious chore!

As we drove up and down, back and forth, we discovered lots of little neighborhood parks. We marked them on the map for future reconnaissance. Since then Beth and the kids have scouted them all out and have thoroughly investigated all of the playground equipment. On our mapping expedition we discovered great picnic spots, places to fish, little off-the-path restaurants, a place to get our car aligned—we found everything! Just a week later a stranger stopped me at the gas station and asked me for directions. I had lived here for two weeks and knew where everything was. I quickly gave him directions to the house he described as having "a green combine set up for demolition derby sitting out front." I could remember exactly where I saw it.

I cannot tell you how much this "getting the lay of the land" has helped us. Even today when a visitor tells us where they live I can tell them I know the house. I am blessed with a photographic memory, and this seems to mean a lot to folks today—that you care and are interested in their lives and where they live. Also, the maps we made were better than the 10-year-old city map we'd been given by the Chamber of Commerce. Had we used their map for our Operation Hope door-to-door campaign we would have missed half the residents. Why? Because Highland has doubled in size in just the last ten years, and all of these new homes are in newly developed and unmapped subdivisions. Since 80% of our church members have lived in Highland less than ten years, had we not used our own maps we would have missed the boat!

Now you have selected your work area, cookware and utensils and you know where everything is. Let's bake some bread.

STEP ONE:
START WITH GOOD FLOUR, CRACK TWO EGGS, ADD MILK AND MIX THOROUGHLY

USE GOOD FLOUR: DEVELOP A QUALITY, PROFESSIONAL IMAGE

Italian cooking demands that one have a respect for and understanding of good foods. This is not the time to buy the cheap stuff—you know, frozen vegetables, dried herbs, that no-name brand of flour that is on sale for almost nothing. I learned an important lesson early in cooking: quality is everything. In baking bread, the flour is the base and literally the backbone of the dish, so choose carefully.

When I bake bread I choose the best flours and grains, the best butter and olive oil, and use only fresh herbs. In a kitchen, perception becomes one-half of taste. When people see fresh, handpicked foods, the choice-of-the-market selections and the best in the cabinets, pantries and drawers, they begin to form a positive mental image.

This is also essential to the new church start. You must choose what will become the base, the image and the perceptions of your congregation. What kind of first impression do you want to make? What do you want to communicate? What do you want to say? Who do you want to speak to? This is where all that homework you have been doing is put to use. Your target group should rise to the front. Be creative! Be unique! Be intentional!

The first thing I did when developing the name Highland Hope was to drop the United Methodist extension of our name. Highland Hope United Methodist Church is listed in the phone directory and on our cornerstone, but rarely anywhere else. We even answer the phone "Highland Hope." The bottom of our stationary in the pre-charter days said, "A Developing Congregation of the United Methodist Church." Today it says, "A United Methodist Congregation." But it is not in our logo or at the forefront of most mailings. Note from our logo, shown in Figure 3-1, that the words "United Methodist" do not appear.

"Why?" I have been asked by many diehard Methodists throughout our conference. The person who asks this probably means, "Why, that church doesn't even say it's a United Methodist church, but they sure are spending our money!" Other sincere individuals believe that "if they would use the Methodist name they would grow—people would just come flooding in." However, if you have done your homework—if you have any understanding of the baby boomers, busters and Xers—you know that:

1. They are disillusioned with the churches of their parents.
2. They left because the church, in many cases, became a museum to tradition rather than a crusader for the faith.
3. The church they left and refused to return to had denominational names tacked on, and as such they bring back negative experiences.

Why start with a strike against you, turning people off before they have even checked you out? Imagine if the Pentagon used most churches' philosophy in dealing with technology, innovation and change in weaponry. We would still be using M-1 rifles, the atom bomb would have been dropped on us by Hitler and I certainly would not have the freedom to write this book, let alone start a church. Remember, as long as it is ice cream, it is ice cream (if this comment makes no sense to you, read the Baskin Robbins illustration on page 16).

Don't get me wrong! I value my church and my Wesleyan background. I choose to be a United Methodist pastor. However, younger generations do not care. They are neither enticed nor impressed by denominational tags. Most of these people have no automatic denominational brand-loyalty. As a matter of fact, their perceptions of a particular denomination might be negative, based on what's in the news, or what happened with a church here or there.

Step One: Start with Good Flour, Crack Two Eggs, Add Milk, and Mix 49

FIGURE 3-1
Highland Hope Logo

In our area, in the last year a male pastor was dismissed, arrested and sentenced to prison for having sexual relations with some teenage boys. This is a tragedy and affront in any church, at any time and in any place. The headlines blaring from the local papers the month I began the PR campaign for Highland Hope proclaimed: "United Methodist Pastor Indicted for Child Sexual Molestation." Imagine with me what some of the kitchen table discussions could have been like as people read the newspaper.

A wife to her husband: "Oh, Honey, you won't believe this. The Methodist pastor in [X] did . . ."

The husband replies: "You know those Methodists, Honey . . ."

As they read on she says, "Hey, guess what."

He responds, "Yeah, what?"

"We have a new church starting in the community called Highland Hope. They look like they're really going to focus on children's and family ministries. Maybe we could get our kids to go there, since our church doesn't have a Sunday school, nursery or children's church. No, wait, it's a Methodist church. Never mind."

I cringed with fear that we would be judged guilty by association, but it seems the link was not established and life moved on.

Why play down the denominational aspect of a local church? The reputation of Highland Hope was founded on our local vision and not our brand label, thus we were not automatically pigeonholed with the whole church. However, many times our United Methodist affiliation is a bonus: for funding, for pastoral appointments, for stability, for steady doctrine, and on and on. I know to denominational diehards this sounds lame but trust me, I have been there. I use the denominational tag when it builds the kingdom of God, and I stay away from it when it tears down the kingdom. Like it or not, today's typical buster, boomer or Xer has low name brand loyalty when it comes to Protestant denominations.

The name "Highland Hope" is presented in a fresh and different way (see Figure 3-1). The logo is distinct and rests on its own vision, mission and philosophy statement. As a result, we created a first impression that shielded us from any preconceived denominational prejudices. Now, you're probably wondering, is this unethical? If you'll notice, our logo (which in full color includes a beautiful sunrise behind the cross) incorporates the United Methodist cross and flame symbol. If being a part of a United Methodist Church is a major factor in your life, the logo will identify us quickly and clearly as a United Methodist place of worship. If you are not denominationally conscious, you will probably simply think, "What a neat design."

With our vision, mission and philosophy statement and our logo in hand, we have the basic ingredients to get started. Remember, use quality, special, clear, repetitive and consistent concepts. I had T-shirts silk-screened with our logo and personally have a dozen polo shirts and even golf hats that sport an embroidered version of our logo. These shirts are made of high quality materials and are in contemporary color schemes. I wear these in the community as often as possible to create a sense of identity for our church. Remember, a new church has no building or land and no long history, just the perception and results of our actions today that set the tone for what Highland Hope will be in the future.

CRACK TWO EGGS: BEGIN YOUR PR CAMPAIGN

The big moment in cooking is mixing the main ingredients. After you crack those eggs, you can't put them back. So have everything at hand—homework done, prep work complete. Now it's time to add your two eggs. In new church development, launching your public relations campaign is like cracking eggs—once it's done, it's done. It cannot be undone, just as Humpty Dumpty could not be put back together again. Much of the success of your church will rely on your communication network, called public relations or PR in the marketing world.

ARTICLES IN LOCAL PAPERS

It started with a simple article I sent to the paper: "Pastor Assigned to Start a New Church in Highland." The article had a picture of me, listed my training, Highland Hope's vision, mission and philosophy and invited anyone interested in finding out more about Highland Hope to contact the church office. The news was out! The eggs were cracked.

From this release in late August until November, a month before our first worship service, we honestly did not do any additional newspaper stuff. I would have liked to have done more, to have promoted our home study groups and other opportunities, but I had, as you can see from our budget in the Appendix, very little money for advertising—actually, none. This is something I would seek funding for in the next start. Local small-town newspaper advertising is very inexpensive, compared to large cities. Plan for it, if you can.

A month before our first worship service on December 3, we began an extensive ad campaign. But first, we sent an article to the paper entitled, "Highland Hope to Begin Worship Services" and followed it with another article in the next three weeks. I learned very quickly that our local newspaper only had two reporters, and that any article with any reasonable information (they never deleted a thing that was important or God-focused), with any pictures that included people, would be printed as often as submitted, *for free!*

Today our goal is to submit at least two or three articles per month. These can be about anything, such as announcing our new Sunday school program. We submitted an article to announce our Hall of Hope[1] award

---

[1] The Hall of Hope is the highest recognition that the church gives to members. As the personalized jade glass award states, it is given "For Outstanding Faithfulness in Providing an Answer for the Hope, 'Well Done, Good and Faithful Servant.' " Highland Hope has established this as a one-time presentation, and the persons or couples who receive the recognition become permanent members of the Hall of Hope. When our first building is completed, the names of all recipients will be placed in a permanent location.

winners and one to honor our senior graduates. We did an article thanking the Jaycees and the community for buying blooming onions at Schweitzerfest. We wrote about everything. Be creative! Use pictures that capture your philosophy. Our pictures were full of kids, youth and adults having a good time together. It would be worth your while to enlist a good writer who understands your plan to be responsible for regularly submitting articles, public service announcements and ads to all the newspapers and radio and TV stations in your area. I did this myself, and had I gotten help I could have done so much more.

Our November ad campaign utilized our logo in conjunction with our philosophy statement. The information was simple, concise and told people how they could "become a part." *We did not use "get involved" language.* We ran the ads like teasers, developing our message more and more each week for a month.

SATURATION CAMPAIGN

As you have probably surmised, I am a doer. I always wrestle with the "being vs. doing" concept from pastoral psychology. I never understood why the two approaches are considered philosophical enemies; I see them as partners. I believe in being. I became a Christian through the unearned, unmerited, matchless grace of Jesus Christ when I invited him into my heart, asked God to forgive my sins, humbled myself and asked God to make me a vessel fitting for his use. I believe in "being" a Christian. But I believe in "doing" the work of a disciple.

In the same way I believe pastors and churches have to pay their dues. You *are* the church! You now need to *do* the work God called you to do—fulfilling the Great Commission. You need to examine yourself, develop your plan and develop your vision. Pastors need to train, study and spend their time as apprentices and journeymen before trying to become self-proclaimed professionals. Does any of this make you perfect or more useful than other mortals? No, it just means you're faithful, available and teachable.[2] These are qualities God can use.

In order to develop a sense of relationship and integrity with the Highland residents, we decided to extend an invitation to every family

---

[2] This is a teaching principle I have heard taught many times in my training work with No Greater Love Ministries, an evangelical men's leadership training ministry.

in the community to be a part of Highland Hope. This we would do in a one day, very intense saturation campaign. We reasoned that if we went to every door in Highland all at once, all of the local churches in the community would get picked on evenly and at least no one would feel left out. Another reason for doing this was that later on we would be doing a Phones for You calling campaign to every Highland resident, and as a former insurance sales person I will assure you warm leads will beat cold calling any day of the week. The brochures we would be planting in September would build much needed bridges so that our phone calls would be better received later in November. (This worked. Many people remembered us from those brochures when we called.) And the picture in the brochure ended my CIA-FBI-covert operations stint, as now everyone I ran into said, "Oh, you're the pastor of that new church!"

I designed a tri-fold, multi-color brochure that simply said on the outside "Looking for Hope?" with our logo below. (I wish I would have had the money to put a couple of these up on billboards, but we were hamstrung financially.) Opening the brochure, one finds the philosophy statement spread around, using bullets, phrases and colored bordering to emphasize the key points. We even included a picture of my family and a brief biography to list my credentials.

The brochure had a simple return postcard which said: "If you would be interested in finding out more about Highland Hope or how you can become a part of one of our home fellowships, please feel free to call or return this self-addressed card with the following information," followed by blanks for name, address, phone number and the best time and day of the week to call. The brochure included a tear-off Rolodex card with our church address on one side and a map to my parsonage/church office on the other. We did not have the money for a prepaid postage return permit, though we had a bulk mailing permit. These are two different things, and each cost money. But in the end I rationalized, maybe justified, that it was better not to include a stamp in this mailing. My goal with the brochure was to be non-proselytizing, providing basic information about a new church available in town, and putting it before the people so they could make their own decisions from there. So I figured if someone was not interested in splurging on a 20- or 32-cent stamp and sticking the postcard in the mail, then they certainly were not going to be interested in the work, cost and effort needed to build a new congregation.

Here is how our Operation Hope campaign worked.

We set a date, and I called on churches throughout the conference to send youth and young adults to Highland on Saturday, September 2, to distribute brochures door-to-door. In some ways this was our debut in the community. Remember those city maps we made earlier? They came in handy here. We divided the workers into squads of eight to sixteen, depending on the vehicle size, and broke them into pairs with a zone map with their territories clearly marked down to two-person routes. (This squad, group and zoning idea came from my experience and training from working with No Greater Love Ministries—apprenticeships do pay off.)

The program was designed to make a strong first impression, for as we all know they are often lasting ones. Over 100 participants, representing more than 15 United Methodist Churches, teamed up into 15 evangelism squads. They acted as mail carriers, delivering a full-color brochure on the Highland Hope project to over 5,000 Highland residences, not just within the city limits but also within a three-mile radius of town. They did this in a little over three hours. By using high school, college, singles and young adult teams we hoped to and, I believe, did establish a youthful and family feel within the community. The Mormons have been evangelizing towns for years with their philosophies, but that day we were there and out in force. We shared a message of HOPE, which only comes through a personal relationship with Jesus Christ. I am so thankful for the efforts of each participant and work mission team for being a part of this historical effort and making Highland Hope a reality. (I plan on doing this again before our first service in our permanent site.)

A few reminders if you use this method. Use young people wherever possible, although it's not a bad idea to utilize your older people in retirement communities. We put everyone in a Highland Hope T-shirt as our gift to them and "made" them[3] wear them that morning so the name would literally be everywhere and clothing would not be an issue. In addition to this, we benefited by sending 100 shirts on the backs of some very excited and thrilled young people to their home United Methodist Churches. I have no doubt this has done wonders for our financial giving from these churches, and I have seen our shirts everywhere, from camp to Six-Flags, on the backs of these kids. Sneaky? No, resourceful! Be multifunctional.

One or two other reminders: do not put the brochures in mailboxes—this is a federal offense. We sent our people out with a generous supply of dollar store clothes pins that work great for hanging the brochures on

---

[3] Be sure to discuss requirements like these with your network organizers before recruiting volunteers so your needs are clearly understood. Then let the leaders interpret the needs to your helpers.

doors. And last, but certainly not least, implore the saturation workers to smile, and to not go inside a home. Simply smile, pass the brochure and bid the residents good day. Baby boomers, busters and Xers love a friendly face, and deplore any kind of sales tactics. The brochure is designed to provide them with all they need to get involved.

During this campaign to reach some 5,000 homes we developed 30 hard leads, ten of which resulted in new families coming to our church. But everyone in our community knew about our church within three hours. People still come to the church today and mention the brochure they received. To count today it has been very effective, but remember, we were working on perception, and that takes time, intentionality and repetitiveness. You cannot start the church on this idea alone, for it would be meager pickin's. (We discuss this later in "Mix Thoroughly.")

MINISTERIAL ASSOCIATION AND LOCAL LEADERS

Now that the eggs have been cracked it's time for formal introductions. Over the next month I scheduled a time to drop in and introduce myself to various community leaders: the mayor, the city manager, the chief of police, the superintendent of schools, etc. With my brochure in hand, and a business card to leave with them, I asked about their community, shared some of the strengths I had noticed and listened to them talk. People love to talk about themselves—that's why authors write books.

I met the local Welcome Wagon lady who visits new residents and asked her how a new church would be able to get a pamphlet and packet of information distributed. She charges local businesses, but does the church promotion as a courtesy. I wrote a special letter welcoming people to Highland, sharing with them a couple of community highlights and inviting them to try the various churches within our community, as well as extending an invitation for them to visit Highland Hope. On all of our new resident stuff, I encourage folks to try all the churches. I know the programs, services and ministries of Highland Hope are second-to-none in meeting the needs of the boomer and buster families moving into the community who are seeking a family-focused church. My thought was that visiting all the other churches would help promote our strengths and would create a stronger loyalty later on when they chose Highland Hope for their own reasons and motives. We are into kingdom expansion, not just doing our own thing. So if new residents end up somewhere else, the welcome letter has still been a success.

I then began to meet the various pastors in town and inquired as to how I could become a part of the local Ministerial Association. This was in September, and by November I was the "Community-Wide All Church Thanksgiving Service" speaker. This was written up in the paper, and I didn't even have to personally write it. What an opportunity!

Let me chase a rabbit for a moment. First, busters, boomers and Xers hate church politics. Many abandoned the church as a result of such battles. No one wins in church politics, except for the enemy, who gets great joy out of a "house divided" (see Luke 11:17). Second, realize you will get disgruntled members from these churches. You will get people whose plan is to remake your church in the image of what they were trying to do in the church they left. This is a fact, and these pastors will want to give you the low-down on these people and on the battle scars for generations past, not to mention the wars amongst the various churches in the community. Many of the pastors will have already heard some of their members saying, "If we were doing what Highland Hope is we would be growing." So their counsel, their perspective, despite their sincerity, is through rose-colored glasses. They will want to tell you how bad these people are and how to be careful, but avoid being distracted by this.

That's why one thing I asked of all the people who helped to begin our first service, and still ask of our church people until this day, is not to discuss negatively another church in our community. Such gossip reminds me of the cola wars. Our strategy is simple: Focus on Highland Hope, and if discussions of what churches did previously begin, simply say, "Oh, well, at Highland Hope we're about doing a new thing!" and move on. Stay above this kind of negative talk. Focus on your vision, mission and philosophy.

ADD MILK: CONNECTIONAL INVOLVEMENT

I like to add a little whole milk or, when I am in the mood, a little buttermilk to my bread recipes. It makes the whole thing blend together better. I have found, in my situation, the support from and relationship to other United Methodist Congregations throughout our conference and beyond is like this milk that improves the bread. We kept them informed via monthly articles in our conference's newspaper and by sending our newsletter to every church that sent us a note of encouragement or said they were praying for us, or anyone who gave us a gift, be it $1 or $2,000. We also sent our newsletter to the conference staff and district superintendents. It seemed everyone knew what was going on at Highland Hope.

In return, we received valuable help from many sources. We were able to use a church van from the O'Fallon UMC on several occasions. In the early days the Troy UMC and St. Matthew UMC let us make and fold hundreds of copies on their machines. Four churches gave us puppets; others sent financial gifts at Christmas, Easter and Thanksgiving. During our Operation Hope campaign, 100 people came from 15 churches. During our Phones for You campaign, five churches came to help us make over 3,000 phone calls in two weeks. Our mentor churches (our God-family) were always there for us, day in and day out, for advice and more.

Whatever problem or issue surfaced early on, there was a United Methodist church or lay person in our area that could help us. Saint Jacob UMC, located five miles from us, loaned us their church basement to act as a nursery during our Home Fellowship Group start-up phase from September to November of 1995. During our first month of services, other UM churches sent representatives to give us crowd support and to greet and send us their best. It was nice not to be a completely independent church—we had the resources of hundreds of churches and ministers all simply a phone call away.

Gaining this support requires a commitment to keeping people informed. People and churches want to help—they just need to know where to go and what to do. This direction needs to come from the pastor. I devoted a good part of the first three months after settling in to the work of public relations. Unfortunately, most seminaries don't train their pastors in this, but, fortunately, I had owned and operated a commercial business and had an undergraduate business degree. The time I had spent in marketing and communications classes was a great help during the start up of Highland Hope.

MIX THOROUGHLY: DEVELOP SEVERAL DATABASES

Have you ever eaten pancakes, bread or biscuits with flour pockets in them? Yuck! Why do those lumps form? They are caused by improper mixing. A general rule of thumb for almost all cooking and baking is that you must mix or stir thoroughly after each ingredient is added. This is a good practice for new church development, too. If you don't mix thoroughly, the lumps might be on your head. Let me explain.

In the interim between leaving Olney in June until our first Sunday worship service at Highland Hope in December, I visited churches throughout our conference. This was part of adding the milk, and part of the covert operations. I slipped in to see what was good, but I was also looking for what was not. I used this time to develop some ideas and concepts to work into the start of Highland Hope. One of the things that concerned me about our local churches and many of our area United Methodist churches is that the people were birds of a feather. Everyone seemed to be from very similar backgrounds. This may be okay in some churches, and I know groups tend to become homogenous over time. But in a church start you do not want all of your eggs to be in one basket, just in case you knock the basket off the counter.

So I established a plan to create several different database groups. If one group, one family or one sector got turned off or disillusioned (after all, the church is not even what I expected from its original conception), then we would only lose a small group and not the whole shooting match. My game plan was to break the names and addresses into five areas. Each of these areas today represents up to 400 names who all still receive our newsletter. My goal is to turn warm leads into hotter ones and, regardless of what happens with these leads, we still have our newsletter sitting in 400 homes waiting for the church to be needed in their lives. Lots of people have heard about us from people who have never attended Highland Hope; they learned about us through our newsletter sitting in the house of a friend or family member.

UNITED METHODIST REFERRAL DATABASE

The first database I began was the United Methodist Referral database. I put a notice in the conference paper, *The Connexion,* for several months like the one shown in Figure 3-2.

Over the next months, in response to this notice, pastors, mothers, grandmothers and friends sent me the names of people who had moved to our area. You never would have thought it, but about 15 names panned out of this, and about eight of those families are in our church today. I developed about 30 names using this list. In each case I sent a letter and/ or dropped by. Regardless of the outcome of my contact, all of these people still get our newsletter today. I figure they will head over when

> **FIGURE 3-2**
> Notice in the Conference Newspaper, *The Connexion*
>
> **Highland HOPE**
>
> **Attention:**
> **All Lay and Clergy Persons in the Southern Illinois Conference**
>
> If you know of United Methodist members, friends or family who have located in the Highland area and would like us to contact them about being a part of Highland Hope, contact:
>
> **Highland Hope, Rev. Troy & Beth Benitone**
> **23 Triland St., Highland, IL. 62249**
> **Office: 618/654-8434 — Home: 618/654-4726**

we meet their comfort level or they have a need. Our goal is to be there extending that invitation: *"Looking for Hope?"*

Some feel that our meeting in a school turns some people off, and I expect more folks will try us as we move to a traditional church location, even though they would learn a lot about the real church of Jesus Christ—the church of relationships—where we are now. This reminds me of a great letter we received. The parent of one of our original families wrote to us about an incident with one of her young children during the early days:

> Dear Troy & Beth,
>
> We just wanted to let you know how much your ministry has meant to us. Thank you for bringing joy back into the worship service for us.
>
> The past year has been somewhat unsettled for us concerning church, and I was beginning to wonder how Kim would adjust. But Sunday afternoon when I was looking for one of Matt's toys, I asked Kim where it was. She said, "It's in the trailer." When I looked puzzled, she said, "I'm playing church, and I put the nursery stuff in the trailer" (the coat closet). I think she has made the adjustment!
>
> Yours in Christ
> Greg, Gayla, Kim & Matt Bruning

If all of us could understand the church in the way this child did, we would be far better off. The church is about people! Not buildings, pews or stuff. But remember, perception is reality! The church doors are always open, and perceptions do change. However, they are often realized through the eyes of small children.

PREMASTER DATABASE

This list was comprised of everyone in the community who, from day one, returned a response card or called after our Operation Hope campaign. It also included anyone our developing home fellowship group participants thought might want information on Highland Hope. This list had about 60 names on it in October of 1995 and is down to about 29 now, in November of 1996. The 30 missing names are mostly all active members now at Highland Hope. Word of mouth works the best when available. These people sought us out.

NEW RESIDENTS DATABASE

This database is the future of our church, and is where we spend about 90 percent of our promotional energy today. We began this database in January 1996, after we had established our worship services. We knew that our strong nursery, children's church program and youth group, along with the many other ministries that we were developing, made us a great community of faith for the boomers, busters and Xers moving into our area at the rate of 25 to 35 families per month. In October 1996, we had 45 new residents. We get the names of new residents from the newspaper; the electric company in our town is city owned, and new residential customers are listed in the paper each month. Not only does the Welcome Wagon lady deliver a brochure packet on our church, but in January of 1995 I started writing a letter to all new residents, inviting them to Highland Hope and including a bulletin and current newsletter. I then added these people to our permanent newsletter file, and they began getting all newsletters and special service mailings. We pick up one or two of these families per month, rather quickly, many a few months after they have settled in. We picked up some more of these people in the summer when we promoted our inaugural VBS. You never know what will click. It's easier to heat warm water than cold, and it sure takes less energy.

> *Why do we send our newsletter to so many people? This true story is one answer to that question:*
>
> Last Mother's Day a lady walked into our church and introduced me to her mother.
>
> "This is my mother, Rev. Troy," she said to me. "Momma, this is my pastor."
>
> I greeted them and they went on in. I consulted with our greeter at the name tag desk and asked my wife and three others who had been around since the beginning, "Who was that?" No one knew. Remember, I was here before everyone else, and I thought I knew every family and child. I thought maybe I had amnesia or a brain aneurysm forming.
>
> I stopped the woman after the service and asked her, "I don't believe I know you."
>
> She said, "Oh, yeah, this is my first time here."
>
> I said "That's nice!"
>
> She said, "Well, I just love it here, and I feel so much a part. See, I just moved here six months ago, and have been getting all of your newsletters. Momma came to town and said, 'Are we going to church?' And so here we are."
>
> She chartered and is an active member of Highland Hope today.

In March we added a second niche by establishing the Hope Brigade. This is a group of foot-soldiers for Christ. I came up with a welcome basket to be delivered by lay persons to new homeowners each month. The baskets are wrapped in a clear floral wrap, and the contents are placed in a nice Pier 1 basket. These are assembled each month and delivered to all new residents as well as to first time visitors to Highland Hope by one of the Hope Brigade team members. These baskets contain two coffee mugs with the Highland Hope logo, each full of candy, a small popular devotion book called *God's Little Instruction Book,* another brochure and a letter from our Hope Brigade crew. These baskets cost us about $10 each, and are wrapped in seasonal wrappings and stuffed with seasonal candies. Our theory is that the pie or loaf of bread that a lot of church Welcome Wagon type ministries send in other communities will be eaten and perhaps forgotten, but free coffee cups sit in cabinets forever or are passed on. In less than a year, our new residential database is up to 295 names. We begin dropping them off a month at a time after 12 months. We would keep it up longer, but the cost has grown too much for us. However, we are planning some future special mailings to all of these names.

Now let's review: We have had the Welcome Wagon deliver church information to new residents; they have received, via the mail, my letter to new residents; and the Hope Brigade has delivered a welcome basket. Focus, intentionality, continuity and consistency are the keys here. No other church in our community is doing anything special for new residents—that's a niche! I imagine our cups will be used a lot by new families over the first months as they are up late painting, moving, decorating and getting their new homes set in order. I hope, when all is said and done, this gift will serve as a reminder to head our way.

PHONES FOR YOU DATABASE

This database was created via the assistance of five area UM churches and several of our faithful early pioneers at Highland Hope. A month before our first service we utilized this campaign, which comes in a package and includes the training, the calling plan and scripts and a follow-up mailing plan. It is a great resource—check it out. However, I feel it had more integrity following up our previous door-to-door/face-to-face campaign during Operation Hope.

We received 161 names from these 3,000 calls, and today we still have about 121 on the list. Some have moved, some have asked to be removed and some are a part of us today. The rest, you ask? We're still warming them up!

ACTIVE DATABASE

The active database is formed from families that started with us or have attended a worship service at Highland Hope. This list was built up to about 125 households; during our charter push we pruned it back to 90 households, getting rid of names of people who had come only one time or had moved away. In a baby boomer, buster or Xer community

> **FIGURE 3-3**
> "We Missed You" Note
>
> **Dear Highland Hope Partner,**
>
> **We hope this bulletin finds you well.** Our registration records indicated you were not in the Sunday morning worship service. We have enclosed a bulletin so that you might stay abreast of the happenings and opportunities for ministry at Highland Hope. Please let us know if you have any special needs or if there is any assistance we can give you or your family.
>
> **We occasionally make a mistake when updating our attendance records; please pardon us if you were at Sunday's worship service and disregard this note.**

people relocate for work quite frequently. As for this list, they were and are still mailed everything, just like members. When a family misses a single service we always mail them a worship bulletin with the announcements insert and the note shown in Figure 3-3.

Yes, all these things cost money and take time to do, but communication is important. Caring for your flock is crucial. These databases are simply another way to communicate passively with our target group.

PHONE TREE

We also have a calling device known as PhoneTree. We named and personified it with the acronym H-O-W-I-E (Hope's Organized Way of Informing Everyone).[4] HOWIE is linked to our church's computer database and can call any sorting of members from the databases, deliver a message and even receive touch-tone responses. We use it to call special groups, leadership teams, setup teams and so forth. It can remind people of time changes, special services and announcements each Saturday. PhoneTree will leave messages on people's machines and can even take a certain number of responses and then shut off. For example, if we need

---

[4] We held a naming contest, and many great acronyms were submitted.

five families to take meals to someone, it will shut off after five responses. What a tool!

I would encourage you to start with it early if you plan to use it, so people will get used to it. I speculate this would not work as well with an older congregation, but in our younger congregation people prefer a one-way, no-strings-attached conversation.

One of the greatest strengths of our church is great communication and dissemination of information via mail, the PhoneTree, bulletin announcements, newsletters and more. Remember, communication equals stronger relationships, and strong churches communicate!

Things are starting to take shape with our bread. Now it's time to add yeast and watch the well-mixed dough rise!

STEP TWO: ADD YEAST AND LET RISE!

ADDING YEAST: CREATING A GOOD OPPORTUNITY TO MINGLE

The part I enjoy the most is adding the yeast, which is the main ingredient in making bread rise. I like adding the yeast because while the dough rises I get to sit on the couch for the next three hours and watch football, baseball or any sport with a ball.

In the last chapter we covered ways to get a promotional campaign going. Now we are going to talk about the time after our first article went out in August until we held our first home fellowship group meeting on September 18 and 19.

As the promotional material was being released, I began contacting all those people from the Methodist Referral Data Base and some of the early people on the Premaster list. I sent each person a letter inviting their families to a picnic at a local park on Saturday evening, August 31. This would be a time to see who would come, to share with them what we hoped to do and to explain the home fellowship groups that would be beginning.

"Bar-B-Que it and they will come!" That day we had 50 adults and about 20 kids representing about 25 households. We had a great evening of eating, ice breaking and then sharing a little on the plan to develop a new church. I told each of the families that we were going to begin Home Fellowship Groups on Tuesday and Wednesday nights beginning September 18 and 19 (three weeks later). They could sign up now, or I would be sending everyone further information, and they could feel free to call and sign up after they were able to check their calendars. Note that this presentation was pressure free! I followed up the next day with a thank you note to each individual who came to the BBQ. Three days later I sent out information on the Home Fellowship Groups. We signed up 22 of the 25 families. Not a bad start!

Timing is everything. This was a great time to get started. See, the summer would have been a bad time, December is too distracting, January and February are too cold and April and May are way too busy with graduation, ball leagues and summer vacations only a month off. But August–September is the time when families with kids regroup, reset their priorities and set their schedules for the upcoming school year. If the church, a youth group or any family-centered ministry is going to get a successful kickoff, the start of school is the window of optimum opportunity.

On September 2, Labor Day, we held Operation Hope. This gave me three weeks before our first Home Fellowship Group and, as people responded to our brochures, I sent them the information and an invitation to take part in one of our first Home Fellowship Groups. One of the keys to the success of the Home Fellowship Groups, which met from 7:00–9:00 P.M. on either Tuesday or Wednesday, was that a nursery was available at a third location, and distractions were out of the house. Families picked a home group, and over the next three months we really got to know and to genuinely like each other. The home groups started looking like one of those happy together, *Thirty Something* episodes.

SET IT ASIDE THREE WEEKS: THE INVITATION TO PARTICIPATE IN HOME FELLOWSHIPS

It takes time to let good bread rise. We allowed three weeks from our BBQ and Operation Hope campaign until each group met together. The groups only grew as *they* invited others. (I think it is essential to place the responsibility for personal evangelization on the flock from the beginning.) This caused our home groups to form some bonds and relationships. The local church was starting to rise quickly, out of my control and beyond my vision. God was doing a new thing!

This three-week interim gave me a chance to pray and listen to God, and utilize the insights I had learned about our families during the picnic in preparing for our first home groups. I believe it also gave these persons something they were looking for in a church—no pressure, just an honest invitation to become a part of something, if they chose. The power, the choice to come was theirs. Their arms were not twisted. I did not beg—I just had a BBQ, told them my vision, gave away some watermelons during an ice breaker game and said, "Let us know what you think."

Some key reminders for church planters: Do your homework! Work hard! Plan, spy, study, check out your community and develop a vision/mission/philosophy statement. Then, when the people come, stand back and let God's Holy Spirit do the work, not the human tongue. When God moves on people's hearts, they will have to answer to God. When our tongues whip their hearts, they will hate us and loathe the God we proclaim to them. I was, and am still, prepared to start over. I am not into a begging ministry, but I am into people choosing relationships and learning to love God and each other. To build these kinds of relationships, this kind of trust, takes words of Hope, Divine Grace, a compassionate heart, a genuine Love and nothing less than the glory of God to give the increase. Had the BBQ failed, I was prepared to keep on, and to try again, because God's people have never stopped going forward. Sometimes, however, we have to put out another "fleece" (see Judges 6, where Gideon tested God by putting out a fleece on two different nights, seeking different results to solve the same dilemma).

One of our vision statements is to build relationships. I have enjoyed our growth from the start of the Highland Launch Team, which basically contained one member of the Highland Hope church and eight conference persons, to the two Home Fellowship Groups of some 50 people, to our first worship service of some 150 local people, which brings us to our current 58 charter families who represent 180 people. Also, we have another 20 households in the process of becoming members in the new year after completing their pastor's classes.

We have never grown so fast that we lost touch with one another. We have stayed at certain levels just long enough so that our people truly know each other. I know as we grow larger this will be tougher, but it is a strength now, and it is something the people treasure. A few occasionally ask, "Shouldn't we be growing faster?" But I find this attitude to be the result of a couple of busters or Xers wanting a crowd to buffer their comfort zone so they will not have to develop personal relationships—something this group often fears. Regardless, I learned to never plan a plan, or push growth to the extent that it outgrows your capacity to provide leadership and assimilate new families into the church. Growth can sometimes become a god of its own.

One of the greatest gifts our congregation has is the ability to assimilate new persons into the life of the church by allowing them to become a part of each other's lives. Our relationships initially were church based/group based, but in less than a year from our first worship service, and given all of the new people moving to our area, there have become many cross-relationships, such as members sharing dinner together, swapping baby sitting and doing non-church initiated or related activities. Highland Hope has helped meet people's needs.

Let the dough rise, take your time and enjoy the breaks in the action, for this is the time when God shines the greatest. The miracle of yeast is that it makes bread rise, and there is very little for you to do but watch and wait.

LET IT RISE: BEGIN HOME FELLOWSHIPS AND ALLOW ROOM TO GROW

Part of baking bread is allowing room in the pan you're using for the proper growth of the dough. In a little over three hours, a small ball of dough will rise to three to four times its original size. This happens because of the space, flexibility and reaction of the fermentation process. The materials I used in our Home Fellowships came from the *Serendipity Series 100*. I tailored them to fit each week and chose good ice breakers out of the series books or additional ideas out of the supplement book that came with the entire kit. After section 100 we did a topical study from the 300 series. These are great small-group tools, as they are designed to engage a group at an increasing level each week. We began each night with a few guitar-led choruses that I taught, hoping to create a time of worship and to prepare them for future worship services. Next, we had refreshments. Then we spent the rest of the evening doing the *Serendipity* material, which focused on gathering, studying, sharing and caring. In this section I want to touch on some of the things we learned about creating successful introductory home groups.

PLAN FOR TWO TO THREE INITIAL GROUPS

When developing your home groups, start with two. It only takes six to eight persons to have a good group. Twelve is a maximum size for one group but could be divided into two subgroups. Our groups grew to about 24 each night, but we subdivided them for discussion into four groups of six. Be sure to rotate the groups. Get the guys together for some male bonding, get the girls together for some ladies' time, divide them by couples at times, by age groups other days and randomly at other times. The goal is to help people get to know each other and to also find some possible bridges or relationship points to cross into one another's lives.

Why not keep to one night and just divide into more groups? First, we had limited space. Second, don't put all your eggs in one basket too soon. Just in case there is a problem or a stink bomb in the bunch, there will be eggs left over. Third, the two groups will allow for more leadership development. In group dynamics I have found whether you have eight in a Sunday school class, 24 in your home fellowship groups or 100 pastors at a conference, a handful of personalities will rise to the top and establish a dominance. I have my own terminology for the players in group dynamics:

1. **The "Pro-Leader"** (Protagonist): The one who rises as the hero of the group, Mr. or Mrs. Got-it-together.
2. **The "Number 1"** (the Protagonist's Assistant): This is the person who supports or agrees with the Pro-Leader. This person is less vocal but takes a side. They have their counterparts. If you've ever watched *Star Trek, The Next Generation,* Commander Riker comes to mind.
3. **The "Con-Leader"** (Antagonist): This person is what some call the "devil's advocate," or the person who opposes the Pro-Leader. This person is sometimes perceived as the group's "pain in the rear" or at least is identified as the person who has the alternative view. If the sky is blue for 98 people, it will be aqua blue for this person, or really gray, or a distortion of some astrological explanation.
4. **"Switzerland"** (The Neutral Party): This person is the one who says we can work it out, let us work to a consensus. This is the other of the 2-in-100 voters. He or she abstains for neutrality and will try to

describe the sky as blue-gray or gray-blue depending on who he or she is talking to.

These types of individuals are part of life, and frankly they are needed to a certain degree within the leadership of the church to review, debate and guard the direction of the church. Since these personalities will surface in most groups, you will want them to be people who are solid in their faith, focused on God and interested in the kingdom and not their egotistical self-justifications. So I encourage you to have two home groups to start, more if you want. We could have gone smaller over more nights, but I wanted to be a part of each group during this phase. Remember, at this stage your job and vision are on the line, and you cannot work every night or you'll have no family support. By having at least two groups, my leadership development doubled. In groups that are large enough you can divide into subgroups of six to eight and still maintain a good small group dynamic, allowing subgroup leadership to take place.

Strong leadership formation is essential. Don't get me wrong—all of your people are important and needed, but this is a great time to learn about the abilities and qualities of your future church leaders. Who's compatible and who's combustible?

PROVIDE MULTIPLE TIMES AND DAYS FOR GROUPS

When I planned the days and times for our Home Fellowship Groups, my basic goal was to reach our target group. I used common sense to make these decisions. Monday is a bad day. Tuesday is good for many as the week is underway. It's not Monday and still a long way from Friday. Wednesday is also a great day; it is the hump day, and people are typically a little more up, for there are only two days to go until the weekend. Most of our community, ball and school activities still respect Wednesday night as a church night, so the competition is limited to the TV and other personal leisures. Thursday I kept reserved in case we needed to add a third group, which we were preparing to do when we decided to have our first worship in December. So instead, Thursday nights became the night our leadership, worship and children's ministry teams met, planned, prayed and prepared for our first services. We settled on Tuesday and Wednesday as the best days for our Home Fellowship Groups, leaving Thursday open for expansion. You will have to do your own homework here and decide what works best for your community.

PROVIDE FREE PROFESSIONAL CHILD CARE AT A NEARBY LOCATION

Unless you have a great building location and the space to have an out-of-earshot, child-friendly nursery, consider offering child care at a separate place. This will be a good practice so that when a church establishes small home groups later they have learned to utilize centralized child care. I have found that having the kids in a separate place helps parents to relax, unwind and enjoy themselves more.

We utilized a separate place and hired a person who works for a local preschool and a teenager to assist her on both nights. They did not just spend the time babysitting, but literally provided a youth group for kids. They had a story time, lesson time, craft time, snack time and a movie time over the two-hour period. The kids all started asking their parents, "Is tonight Bible study?" Our home group nights became a positive night for the kids almost immediately and a plus to the parents, who were giving up a valuable night they could have spent at home.

Baby boomers, busters and Xers are typically double income families. Both parents work, kids go to school, day care and/or preschool. They commute to work, come home only to have to race kids to ball, dance, and this or that activity or lesson. Asking them to spend two hours of one of their few evenings at home in the small group means they lose family time, which is a valuable commodity. So at Highland Hope we try to be sure our time together is quality driven and a plus to their week. We want families to feel it is time well spent. This is a rule of thumb for all of our activities, and nursery care is provided for all our adult activities that are not age appropriate for children.

Don't skimp on the child care! Offer it, but respect those parents who choose to use their own. Remember our vision: "to build trust." It may take time, but it can be done. Also, do not charge parents for this service—incorporate it into your start-up budget. In my first three months, with the exception of inviting families to bring a side dish to the BBQ, the start-up budget covered the nursery, the snacks for home fellowship and the materials cost. This is a time when money is not an issue. Don't be mooching for a dollar here and there—it's the "wine and dine time." This is a time when we are showing them our priorities, and those priorities are strong relationships, trust and Jesus Christ, not nagging them about money to meet expenses.

Invest now and it will come back. "Give and it will be given to you" (Luke 6:38). This is all part of the promotional process. There will be plenty of time for people to do their share later. You can't imagine how many times over the three months people said, "Can I bring something?" or "Please let me help with the baby sitting." We always said, "No, we won't have it, you just relax and enjoy this time apart. There will be plenty of time for that in the future." People were shocked. They were amazed, some even relieved. No hidden cost, no prodding for this and that. No worry for some about having to get home in time from work to fix snacks for Home Fellowship. All they had to do was come. The kids loved it, and they even had a free baby sitter. They had no excuses not to come!

EXPAND GROUPS SLOWLY

Once a group hits 24 members (four groups of six) start a new group, but wait to have at least 12 to begin the new group. Remember that waiting is a virtue in baking good bread.

If your groups grow, don't expand them too quickly. A little waiting and anticipation by some will be okay. Don't water down, slash or reorganize your existing groups in the middle of a study series just to cram in another group. Let your starting groups complete their relationship development, which will take six to eight weeks minimum, before spinning off a new group. This is how this material is designed. To do this any sooner will cause what I call "the touchy-feely syndrome." This is the eby-geebees that boomers, busters and Xers get when things get overwhelming and too many unknown people are all seemingly trying to touch them and invade their space in these small groups. Wait to start your next group until you have about eight to sixteen people. Then move forward with a new group, ready to learn and build relationships together.

Hey, we're off! When the small groups start and the discipling begins, realize that the ship is afloat. But beware, the barrier reef is coming up—the first worship service. However, fear not, for God is watching over you and Jesus Christ, the Captain of the Host, is at the helm. Sailing should be safe until morning.

STEP THREE:
PUNCH IT DOWN

PUNCH DOWN: SEE WHAT'S FLUFF AND WHAT'S STUFF

After the bread completes the first rising, it's time for the masculine side of the sport of baking Italian bread—punching it down. It's like boxing a marshmallow. Taking the cover off, you punch the bread down, deflating it, flipping it inward, checking it for any lumps and areas of concern before putting it back down to rise another couple of hours.

In our church's development there was a phase between beginning our home fellowship groups in September and holding our first worship service on December 3, when it was time to punch it down. This chapter may be brief, but pay attention, because lumps in the dough will mean bigger lumps in the finished bread.

In new church development, when people hear there will be something new in town, three groups of people will jump at the opportunity. I call them "Flakes, Fruits and Nuts."

THE FLAKES

Flakes are the ones you want to be the most concerned about—people who flake, jump, bounce, float, skip or whatever you want to call it, from church to church, seeking a pastor who will "speak to" them, a church that will "meet my needs" or a church that will let them take control. They are looking for the First Church of "Do as I Want Done." They come with preconceived ideas and a dream of destroying their previous church and building this one in their image. It's like a bad version of Dallas with Bobby and J. R., brothers who are trying to destroy one another.

> **THE CHURCH IS WHERE WE WORSHIP, AND WORSHIP IS LOVING GOD AND EACH OTHER.**

How do you handle these people? Well, most of them, in my case, were cut off at the pass when I refused to engage their pedigree of previous pastoral complaints. These are the things flakes live for. I simply invited them to be a part of our fellowship and let them know that Highland Hope was doing a new thing, and we never varied our vision. We simply invited people to become a part. Most of the flakes floated off to another church or drifted down the road after they found they could not control this church. I pray that one day these people might settle down and realize that the church is where we worship, and worship is loving God and each other.

THE FRUITS

The next group are the fruits. These are not fruity as in nuts, these are the sun-ripened, naturally sweetened, vitamin enriched and productive people who inquire about the new church and are seeking a place to share their gifts, talents and abilities in God's orchard. At Highland Hope from day one we have had a tree full of fruit. We are blessed with so many talented people: teachers, bankers, real estate agents, agricultural specialists, craftsmen, carpenters, music teachers, accountants, phone repairmen, industrial workers, CAD designers, police officers and so forth. From day one until December 3, we found that within our small but faithful developing group we had gifted individuals equipped to fill all the necessary ministry functions to start a healthy and vibrant church. These people could excite and challenge even the deadest of pastors.

Let me journey ahead a few months for an important reflection. As we moved into our sixth month of worship, I noticed a few of these fruits were getting bruised. In reviewing my actions with them, I found several of the younger ones needed a break. Even a fruit tree, such as an apple tree, needs a winter of 700 hours of freezing weather to grow dormant, to rest and prepare for a new season. Upon noticing some sense of burnout, I adjusted some of our ministries, added to our volunteer depth, asked new members who were ready for leadership to step up, and on and on. Things got better and bruises healed. Some things just needed adjustment, and some individuals just needed a change in ministry setting. Four of the women (one of them being my wife) had been leading our children's church since our inception. They had never heard me preach, let alone attended a full worship service. Imagine their burnout! They were suffering from malnutrition. I thank God for each of these people who went above and beyond the call of the duty to get our church off the ground. They have taught me to watch for burnout and monitor my fruit trees better in the future.

THE NUTS

Finally, the third group are the nuts. I love nuts. I love fruit. Both are healthy. A church can't handle too many nuts, however. Nuts challenge the status quo. Nuts are willing to push us to the edge. They see ahead and are willing to trust God, take risks and push it to the utter extreme of the envelop. Pastors appreciate a few nuts, but they are also high maintenance.

Let me suggest that you pick out the nuts early and build a relationship with them up front that allows you to dialog with them, encourage them and harness them in a way that will be constructive. By having a good relationship you will be able to be honest. I personally am a nut. I have thousands of great ideas, thousand of concepts, schemes and plans floating around in my head at any one time, and unfettered I would move heaven and earth, no matter what the cost, to fulfill my dreams. I love the labels on the sides of those cans of mixed nuts that say "less than 1/3 peanuts." This means the other 2/3 are good nuts—cashews, Brazil nuts, smoked almonds, etc. I don't know how accurate this is; have you ever tried counting them? I am more like 99% peanuts with an occasional jewel popping up every now and then. But God gave me a wife who can pick out the good nuts and "can" the others without destroying my ego.

As you spend time in your home fellowship groups, get to know your people and build relationships. Learn to work with the flakes, grow the fruit and sort the nuts. Remember, each of these people are precious in God's sight. He has sent them your way to teach you something about yourself or to help the church grow in some aspect. After all, God has a plan for their lives, too. In this phase, listen to people talk and watch them walk. See what's fluff in their lives and what's stuff. These observations, prayers and the leading of the Holy Spirit will be instrumental in designing the leadership matrix of your developing congregation.

SIFT OUT THE TROUBLEMAKERS

When you punch your bread down, feel for lumps or foreign objects. I have been known to occasionally leave a dough lump unmixed in the batter, so I just pinch it out if I find it at this stage. As you begin to develop some rapport with your people in the home fellowship phase, trust the feeling in your gut, trust the leading of the Spirit. If a personality or attitude tends to be squelching the temperament, spirit and flow of your group on a routine basis, be prepared to sift it out.

There will be people, at times, who have theologies and ideologies that will utterly surprise you. Remember, never compromise in the area of doctrine, never compromise by backing off the Great Commission or neglecting the commandment to love God and each other. Watch out for those who say, "It would be better if we didn't do this or that." This is often the result of one feeling uncomfortably stretched. These persons are probably used to facing such challenges by making others more uncomfortable and pushing their opponents to return the environment to one friendlier to their perspectives.

Here is how I try to work with such individuals. First, when you teach or talk with them in a group only answer questions you are ready to answer. Don't let them trap you with off-the-wall questions you haven't thought through or prayed about. They may be trying to pigeonhole you into their camp. I guarantee they have thought their plans out, so be sure you do the same. In many cases, I asked people to let me think about that concept for a while, and then either answer their concern in a later group session or, if needed, meet with them privately at a later time. However, I always make it a point to respond.

Second, if their questions and comments get to be a group disturbing tactic or they become routine "Con-Leaders/Devil's Advocates," you need to plan to meet them either informally (if you believe there would be a chance to discuss your concerns), or formally, if you feel that you need to get together for some theological discussion. Remember, never argue. I love to debate in private, one-on-one sessions, but I never raise my voice in defense. To do the latter implies insecurity, but calmness implies confidence and faithfulness to Christian doctrine. God's Word is the only Rock to stand on when sharing the Hope of Christ. Never, never give in on doctrinal issues. They are not yours to cave in on, they are the church's. Remember, when you cave, every future pastor will have to deal with these persons in the light of your retreat.

Third, if these individuals become too destructive to the group and conversion does not seem likely, don't be afraid, as I have done before, with love and a true Hope, to remind them that they came here by their own choice and, based on their theological views, they might feel happier and be more constructive to the kingdom in another church. Sounds harsh? It is. This approach should be used only as a last resort. These troublemakers can consume, detour and totally distract a whole church group in this early development phase. An established church might be able to spend more time working toward a conversion, but the pace of new church development makes it a very difficult and time-consuming problem. I only go to this extreme when I feel they are becoming contagious. As long as they are seeking the truth, I can go to the wall.

More churches must start sifting out the troublemakers, because in so many churches I visit the church is being wagged by these persons, like a tail wagging a dog. Many pastors are weak in confronting these persons because these troublemakers tend to be well educated intellectuals, not to mention they believe fiercely in their argument. They will test *you* to find out whether you are all fluff and no stuff!

ROLL INWARD: GATHER YOUR CORE TOGETHER

As you complete the punching fest with your dough and finish sifting out the lumps, roll it inward a couple of times to gather the core together. Place the dough under the bowl and *let it rise again.*

This is the fun part. You have now stereotyped everyone ... it sounds horrible, doesn't it, but unfortunately, to develop your leadership matrix, you will have to make some decisions based on your observations. Trust in prayer, your calling, your training, your guts and your vision. But, don't forget weekly prayer, fasting and repentance, for there will be many mistakes made. Jesus was patient with his disciples, and his

Grace, Mercy and Love will always be there for you. Take your observations, selecting out the choice fruits and nuts, those with the right stuff, and spend time apart with them. Jesus developed special relationships with some of the disciples, notably Peter, James and John. Take these different people out to lunch, to dinner or to a ball game. Get them outside the church scene. Are their actions on Monday the same as on Sunday? Does their talk still fit with their walk? Share your visions with them and listen to theirs. By now there should be some harmony forming. As your leaders emerge, start bringing these groups together and see what kind of synergy develops.

A colleague who read this manuscript in its formative stages asked, "If the people had not come together, did you have a Plan B?" There is no question that the Holy Spirit should be given the credit for bringing the right individuals with the right gifts together so quickly, but had it not been so, I would have waited on God. I would have spent more time developing home groups and expanding the early base. If the group developed, yet I still had need of a specific person in children's ministry or music ministry, I could have worked through two nearby Methodist colleges to find persons interested in short-term ministry opportunities.

Be patient, trust in God's Spirit, and don't forget that God is the author of creation. Consider seeking creative options, ideas and paths, but regardless of method, wait on the Spirit. You will know when, if God has called you to be a church planter.

STEP FOUR: LET IT RISE AGAIN!

WHAT TO DO, WHAT TO DO?

After you punch the bread down, it's time to let it rise again. This will be the final rising before making it into loaves for the oven. As your leadership is developing, your groups are expanding and the Spirit of God is beginning to gel. Now it's time to begin doing the ground work for the next step, the first worship service. Use your time wisely. You don't want to start formal worship services too soon. You need to allow plenty of time for your leadership to rise. However, you do want to pick the right time of the year. Those are some of the issues we are going to take a look at while the bread is rising again.

VISIT OTHER SUCCESSFUL CHURCH MODELS WHILE YOU WAIT

After our leadership team began to take shape in late October and November, we began talking about starting our own worship service. What to do? I decided to take our leadership team to visit several churches in our area. I picked churches that were successful, or that had aspects of ministry that might benefit the development of our own worship service. You will undoubtedly need to design and create a worship service that fits the needs, tastes and gifts of your congregation, but you can glean some ideas from other churches.

Over a four-week period, fifteen to thirty of us pioneering Highland Hopers, visited four area churches. Churches with strength in contemporary upbeat worship. Churches with a Wesleyan flavor. One church with an excellent family life center, and two of which had experienced tremendous growth in a rural setting. Each church helped us to learn more about who, what and how we should be about the business of providing a top-quality, Spirit-led and God-centered celebration time.

VISIT UNSUCCESSFUL CHURCH MODELS

Don't hesitate for a moment to take your congregation to a church that is not doing well, not reaching its target audience and is at the other end of its life cycle. This will allow them to see extremes, and that congregations do have alternatives. Bishop Handy taught me this all so well in his class. Though we studied the fastest growing churches in the Atlanta area, he had us analyze and talk with the pastors in declining and shrinking congregations as well. In 100 percent of these visits to unsuccessful churches, most members thought all was well. Others thought everyone else was wrong. All of them had lost touch with the people Jesus died for in 1995, 1996 and until his return.

Jesus knew how to relate to his environment, the people and their context. The successful models we visited do this well; unsuccessful models don't. Our people were able to see the difference and have had the privilege of shaping a church based on a good foundation of prayer and some excellent reconnaissance work. They have designed a worship experience that meets the needs of our Highland residents yet remains faithful to God's Word and our vision.

Do your homework, and have the congregation do theirs as well. If a picture is worth a thousand words, then a visit by your people to successful and unsuccessful church models will be more valuable than reading or sitting through hours of information on church growth. They will be able to see it and experience it.

GET OUT THE COOKING STONE: THE QUADRILATERAL OF SUCCESSFUL CHURCH DEVELOPMENT

When the bread is rising for the last time, it is my cue to dig out the cooking stone. I love to bake pizzas and breads on it. It makes the crust hard and crisp, and reminds me of the stone hearths used to bake bread in my family's homeland of Italy. The cooking stone is the foundation, the base on which good bread is baked. This brings us to the quadrilateral of successful church development, my own design. In the Wesleyan tradition, the Wesleyan Quadrilateral is the base on which John Wesley taught sanctified believers to live. The Wesleyan Quadrilateral was a formula for interpreting good Christian doctrine. It was accomplished by combining four things: the study of church tradition, personal experience, intellectual reason and the Holy Scriptures. In the Wesleyan Quadrilateral, these four points were not of equal importance. The Word of God, Scripture, stands first and foremost. But, building upon the foundation of Scripture, tradition, reason and experience can be used to interpret the Bible to the believer in the light of modernity.

I have found there is also a quadrilateral in developing a successful and viable congregation that meets the needs of today's Christian family. The "Benitone Quadrilateral" is based on these four areas: the nursery care team, the children's church team, the greeting and hospitality team and the music ministry team.

NURSERY CARE

I will not say this is at the level of Wesley's statement that Scripture was primary in his Quadrilateral, but I will say that if the nursery care is not excellent and does not make a good first impression, then one leg of trust has been knocked out before a buster or Xer family with small children even hits the pew. In the old days, mothers held their kids in church. This was not a perfect situation when the child was lively, but there were often more grandmothers and aunts and kindly older women in the church who would take a turn with a squiggling toddler. This has totally changed since my first appointment in 1990. Over the last ten years two-income families have become the norm among the busters and Xers. Many of the new families in Highland Hope do not have relatives in the congregation or in the community. Kids are raised in day-care and preschool, by baby sitters and others. Youngsters are more rowdy, perhaps because they need a high energy level to survive in these more competitive environments. Right or wrong, like it or not, whatever the reasons—this is a fact. So, if parents of young children come to church and the nursery does not look like their day-care nursery—meaning it is child friendly, clean, safely equipped and professionally staffed—they will not be back. Our staff workers wear beige smocks with our logo embroidered on them, to protect them from spit-up and to identify them. In the summer, they wear our Highland Hope T-shirts.

Our nursery, although it is portable, still has two Jenny Lind cribs and a portable crib that folds up and stores in a bag for overflow days. We roll out fresh carpeting on the school floors for the toddlers. Our toy boxes have no wooden or metal toys, only plastic, washable items that are sanitized regularly. We provide large toys, riding toys and bouncing toys. We built a rolling kitchen cabinet with a counter top that stores all the changing equipment and nursery supplies and serves as a great baby-changing station. We even have a swing and two glider rockers. A TV-VCR combo unit and over 50 children's Bible stories and sing-along tapes enhance youngsters' listening and spiritual development. All of this is portable, new, clean and child safe.

One distinct advantage to hiring your nursery staff is if there are problems, the termination of a worker does not affect a member of the church. We have staffed our nursery at Highland Hope from day one with trained day-care and preschool teachers who have early childhood development training. Why? We want the best for our kids. Our staff members are more than babysitters. They love and care for our kids. We do provide, in addition, two rotating adults who are church members, one scheduled and one on standby each week. The volunteers work one Sunday per month, and it is the same Sunday each month, so that they can develop relationships with the kids. Our nursery workers know our kids and have relationships with them, and the parents trust them.

Hire the appropriate people. We use a ratio of one adult to four kids, so we have, as a norm, the two staff workers and one volunteer for check-in and check-out assistance before and after the worship service. The volunteer stays in the nursery the entire time if the number of babies grows to 8–12. If we go beyond 12, we call in the standby volunteer. Beyond 16 children, we find a nonscheduled volunteer worker or utilize one of our Andrew's Ministers/Greeters.

Hiring professionals will ensure that good ethics and procedures will be followed. Child care issues can be upsetting to mothers, and our nursery care workers are properly trained to alleviate those fears. Provide a professional nursery. Don't skimp here. Our kids are our most precious assets. We communicate that to our parents and they treasure it.

CHILDREN'S CHURCH

The second area, and probably one of the greatest drawing cards of our church, is our children's church program, which we call "Kids' Kingdom." We realized that we needed to have it going from day one. It is our hope that our children will learn to love and worship God. By providing a service designed to fit their learning levels and attention spans, we communicate to them the importance of learning about God.

The children in our congregation start in the main worship service. We want families to have a time to worship together. As we do our announcements and sing our upbeat "Songs of Praise" the kids take part. We have a special Kids' Kingdom Sermon in the chancel area, not to show them off but to allow them to have their own time with me as their pastor or with a lay person within our church. We never rush our Kids' Kingdom Sermon as we enjoy this time of learning together and spend a significant amount of time with them. We use the David C. Cook *We Worship Jesus* curriculum, which has a sermon idea book, unless I have another alternative for a special occasion. By using the plan's sermon, it fits in with what they will do in their children's church program over the next 45 minutes.

Our kids leave our service following their sermon time and go to their worship area. They start off singing in their room, which has an altar, a puppet stage, seating, an overhead projector, tables and all the things a mini-church should have. They learn Scripture memory verses. They take up their own stewardship offering. Next, they move to an age-appropriate group and work in table teams led by our four children's church teachers, using the curriculum. During this time they do crafts, hear the Scripture stories and more. All of their experiences here will be used in their final worship time. Following the table time they enjoy a puppet ministry, led by our fifth and sixth graders. They finish with their own call to worship, the Scripture reading, a review of the lesson and a recap of my sermon that day.

Our children's church has captured more young hearts and convinced more parents that Highland Hope is for them than any other ministry in our church. Our children's church staff meets monthly, reviews the services and the kids' needs, talks through any problems, plans for the next month and even plans Saturday outings such as bowling and special trips during the summer months. This group is led by a lay-volunteer director, three more teachers in addition to the director and a puppet ministry coordinator. They also have four substitutes, one for each class, in order to maintain continuity. We use regular volunteers in the children's church, the same substitutes when needed and the same rotation in the nursery to ensure that our kids feel secure and develop relationships with their adult leaders. Because so many kids in our church have dual homes, we want the church to appear very stable. We never rotate weekly, but change adult leaders on a six month or annual rotation schedule in an effort to prevent kids from feeling passed around.

One of the greatest success stories at Highland Hope is that I am not the catalyst behind any of these ministries. The creation, policies and development of these ministries belong to the people of Highland Hope. I give input to the directors when asked or when I feel it is needed, and they do the rest of the planning. They own it, they care about it and they have a heart for God in doing it. We are blessed at Highland Hope with people who love and care for children beyond measure.

GREETING TEAM

One of the key things our group discovered as we visited unsuccessful models was that it seemed they didn't know or care that we were there. Everyone in our group noticed that.

The name of our greeting ministry is the "Andrew's Ministry," after the disciple Andrew who was the first person to win someone for Christ. They handle all of our greeting and ushering responsibilities. There are six volunteers assigned each week, and they do the same Sunday each month for a minimum six-month stint, which helps them become familiar with the people. The six people are assigned to three areas:

- Two people are at the main doors.
- Two people staff the name tag table.
- Two people are in the hallway handing out worship bulletins and helping with coats.

Boomers, busters and Xers do not like the pastor to put a spotlight on them in the middle of a worship service, asking them, "Would you stand and introduce yourself to us, and here is your BIG RED BUTTON that says: I am a Visitor. Let's give our visitors a hand—(applause)." Would you come back after that treatment?

People in these age groups want to slip in and, at most, be gently pointed in the right direction and allowed to fit/blend in and slide out unscathed. If they come back the next week, they probably felt comfortable. So how do you greet people who don't like the spotlight? Well, this requires planning and common sense. What are these people used to? They are used to parking valets, they are used to people holding a door, they are used to receptionists, they are used to coat checks and the various people they pass daily. So we have used the philosophy at Highland Hope that "we don't mug visitors."

In the rain, all of our members and visitors are met by greeters in the parking lot with umbrellas to escort them in. As you come to the doors, a person holds the door with a smile and says, "Good morning!" Perhaps you're thinking—this is canned. No way! The people at Highland Hope want and have the heart to build a church, and really like to build relationships. This is called the gift of hospitality in the Bible, and they are truly blessed with it.

After entering our door, the hospitality desk is right there, and another friendly face says, "Good morning! Can I get you a name tag?" You're thinking, "Name tags? They're pushy, aren't they?" At Highland Hope everyone wears them, so they are the norm and you don't feel weird. (Also, many visitors will be used to wearing name tags at business and professional gatherings.) A sign on the table says: "Wearing your name tag is your gift to others." We have plastic clip-ons, with laser-printed name inserts on a specialized Highland Hope name tag stock. Visitors are given a handwritten one, but there is always a laser-printed, permanent name tag there the next week to surprise them when they return. Many times people who return the second week say, "Oh, it's printed, already! Wow. How did they do that?" Doing this tells them they are noticed, cared for and needed. People will sometimes call us ahead in the event friends or family are coming so we can preprint a name tag for their visiting guest. But, if visitors say "no thanks" when the name tag is offered, not a word or odd glance is given. No arm twisting, guaranteed.

After moving on they are told "good morning" again as they are handed a bulletin or offered help hanging up their coats. Though we are meeting in a school, we still have nice laser-printed magnetic signs all over, pointing out the directions to the restroom, nursery and children's church. Signage is important. We use real estate signs on the school corners and entrances with our logo on them. These signs are totally portable, and we use them for other functions at homes, for picnics and so forth.

Without torturing anyone, a family is greeted, told good morning and is able to find help in three locations if needed, but the choice and power to open up is given to them.

Finally, our Andrew's Ministers are responsible for lighting the candles, putting the registration pads out during the song service, taking up the offering and helping with Communion.

In our church we dress for all styles. I typically wear my Highland Hope staff shirt and a pair of Dockers in the pulpit, only donning a suit on rare occasions. I try to demonstrate, as the pastor, the freedom to come as you are. Our greeters do the same. Some dress in suits or dresses, others in casual wear. Over half of our congregation has Highland Hope polo and denim shirts, and they are common, too. So when you walk in, you will be dressed appropriately, and you will be reassured of that quickly.

It's hard to measure the effects of our Andrew's Ministers, but I can assure you that if they did not do their job, we would not grow. Church growth statistics say that people make up their minds to join a church in the first 15 minutes. That means the greeters are a lot more important than the preacher, who will not be on for another 45 minutes. If they do their job faithfully, with a heart for God and a love for God's people, then I will get a chance to do mine.

MUSIC MINISTRY TEAM

Our music is beyond my wildest expectations. This was my greatest concern coming to Highland. I play a lousy guitar and cannot sing. My wife, Beth, doesn't play or sing, and I had no clue where we would go for this need. In our Home Fellowship Group alone we were blessed with two choral music teachers and three women with choir directing experience. All are excellent musicians, and one is a phenomenal vocalist who has sung in the Crystal Cathedral and has the voice of an angel. We very rarely use a track tape, because between the gifts of our keyboardist and pianist and the quality sound of our Kawai Keyboard, our music is all original and quite awesome. In addition, we have people who can play guitars, flutes, violins, trumpets, trombones and xylophones. We have an accomplished pianist who plays by ear, and other musicians available. We have lots of talent. These people have all worked and developed our music ministry in consultation with my hopes and vision, utilizing their talents to create music appropriate for our context. They formed our Hope Ensemble to sing and lead the music, and even set up orchestrations for special services and occasions. I would say more about this ministry, but what do I know—I am still amazed myself. Remember—God is in control!

In my case, I was blessed with lay people gifted in each of the four vital areas—nursery care, children's church, greeting and music—after only a few months. I believe this was none other than God's divine providence. But I will assert that quality vision, mission and promotional planning will draw quality people. Had I not been blessed so soon with such gifted persons I would have stayed in the home group phase longer, working toward continual growth and seeking people with gifts in these four areas. A few areas such as nursery workers and musicians could be hired staff, depending on your budget.

SET THE TIMERS: ADD THREE WEEKS TO THE DATE YOU THINK YOU WILL BE READY FOR YOUR FIRST SERVICE

The title of this section says it all. Baking bread always takes longer than it should because . . . well . . . I open the door too much, so I always add another two or three minutes. When we were planning the dates for our first worship service, at first impulse I picked the earliest date possible. But, upon looking at the calendar, I realized that the date I had selected fell during deer season. Many of our men made annual pilgrimages that were planned for decades in advance, and they would be gone. So that date was a bad idea.

Then let's try the next week, I reasoned. Oh, it was Thanksgiving weekend. People are tired and foundered from the turkey day feast. Others would still be out of town. Of course an existing church would have a service the Sunday after Thanksgiving, but since we hoped to attract as many first-time visitors as possible to our first worship service, this date was no good. Then we looked three weeks later—December 3, 1996. "Oh, it's advent." As I studied my liturgical calendar, my eye lifted, I bowed to praise God and I said, "This is the date, print the invitations." December 3 was the first Sunday of Advent, of which the theme is HOPE. God is REAL good!

ARE YOU SURE YOU'RE READY?

I implore you, I beg you to ask the question: "Are we ready to worship?" Be honest. Don't start too soon, because once you start you can't stop. Worship is not a one-hour event, it is a weekly production that takes a lot of energy, a lot of dedicated people and the right equipment. It's hard to start over. Be sure you're ready! Then do it with class and quality.

FIRST IMPRESSIONS ARE LASTING ONES!

Do it with quality. Purchase and put together all of the worship equipment. Hold a rehearsal with the equipment, practice, work out the kinks. How will you move, store and set up your equipment? Remember, don't skimp here. Feel free to improvise, but don't cut corners. We even bought artificial plants and trees to wheel into the school, literally transforming the school auditorium into a house of worship. First impressions are lasting ones, so "be prepared," as the Boy Scout motto says.

The Appendix includes a list of the initial worship equipment that we purchased and set up each week.

TIMING IS EVERYTHING: DECIDE WHEN TO DO IT

Wait until you're ready, do it first class and be sure to pick the right wave. Ever been body surfing in the ocean? You swim out, watch for a swell, and as it comes to you, you begin to swim, putting your body into it and . . . nothing. You missed. The goal is to hit the swell of the wave as it rolls and to be caught in the momentum of the water and, with your hands out front, to glide or, in my case, be hurled on the water like a surfboard. It's a great thrill, but it is embarrassing to miss the wave as your friends surf off on top toward the beach while you're treading water in the deep.

In starting a church there are two major windows. The first is in September, when school starts and families are resetting their sched-

Step Four: Let It Rise Again! **89**

ules, as discussed in a previous chapter. And there is December, the first Sunday of Advent and the beginning of the Christian calendar year. Advent is the time of the year when even the most stubborn of hearts turn toward the reason for the season, Jesus Christ. People get in the church mood at this time.

What's wrong with November? It might be okay. How about January or February? Fine in some places, but too much snow and ice in others. The cold might cause your first service to be snowed out, or your next two or three to be so poorly attended due to the weather that your people lose heart. How about Easter? Could be done around Holy Week but, remember, summer is coming, and the let down for us after starting in December was hard enough, let alone going right into the vacation season after only a few weeks to stabilize your new worshipping congregation. The main point here is for you to examine your community, the calendar, your weather trends and the schedules of your people. You need to have at least six to eight weeks, preferably three months, to establish a regular attendance before hitting any seasonal or regional attendance slumps. "When to do it and when not to do it?" will be questions you must pray about, discuss and think through very carefully. Homework is still required!

STEP FIVE:
FORM IT INTO A LOAF!

DECIDE WHAT STYLE THE LOAF WILL TAKE: PLAN YOUR ORDER OF WORSHIP

Things are coming together great! It's almost time to see your work take shape. Take the dough, divide it into the desired number of loaves, style it the way you wish and into the oven it goes. With this dough you can make individual sized loaves, huge loaves, round breads, oval breads, long breads, bread sticks. . . . You can make artistic cuts in the bread for special designs, and so forth. When Highland Hope was ready for its first worship service, we had to determine what kind of loaf God wanted us to make!

WITH FIZZ

Highland Hope's target group contains people whose fast-paced lives need to slow down a little so they can hear God—but we don't want to put them to sleep! The key is to develop a service with **FIZZ**!

An incredibly aggravating event occurs in the beach air. Every time you pour yourself a nice cold Coke or Pepsi it happens. Before you sit down and take the first sip, your drink has already lost its carbonation. It's syrupy and sweet, but has no **FIZZ**! I don't know what happens—maybe it's the moisture or the salt in the air—but yuck!

Don't develop a "yucky" service. In other words, don't be cute, sweet or syrupy, and don't be boring, outdated or trendy. Build a service with **FIZZ**, a service tailored to fit your target group. Ignore the traditional or standard services of other churches of your brand name in the area. Use your homework, the leading of the Holy Spirit, the abilities and personalities of your target group and the ideas of your leadership as you plan a service that fits you. One comment often heard at Highland Hope is that time goes unheeded when we worship. Whether our service runs one hour or one and a half hours, people rarely notice. The service moves with a nice flow, and leads people in preparing their hearts and minds to develop a deeper relationship with God and each other.

BE Flexible

Have some stable elements in your worship. Develop a consistency. It might take time, a few months or even a year (we are still making adjustments), but the key is finding your tempo. Occasionally, however, make weekly changes. For example, last week we began a two-part series where we began the service with a song of praise and watched selected clips from the movie *Rudy;* then I shared about "Having a Heart for God." It was a totally different service for us. Why did we do it? To be different. This creates an atmosphere where there is a sense of anticipation, where no one knows whether the routine will always be routine. Plus, it creates the precedent for me to make other adjustments in our service as we change. I hate those words of doom and death: "We've always done it that way." Be flexible and plan **flexibility.**

HOLD ON TO Tradition

Listen to this. Hold on to some tradition.

I didn't say die for tradition, and don't confuse tradition with doctrine. But avoid the traditional "Stand up, sit down, stand up, sit down . . . fight, fight, fight!" You know, pray, stand up; announcements, sit down; hymn, back up; amen, down; offering, up; special music, down; Gospel reading, up; sermon, down . . . You know what I'm talking about!

Our service flows in three phases—a time of preparation (songs of praise), a time of prayer and study (joys and concerns, Scripture readings) and a time of celebration (a message of Hope and a time for response). Sermons focus on Hope, Mercy, Grace and Love—the good news! People can get the bad news in the newspaper or on the evening news. In September 1997, we changed our service to a considerably more contemporary format, and went to a music style that is enriched with jazz, rock and rhythm and blues. Why? To keep up with the waves. (A sample worship bulletin appears in the Appendix.)

So why keep some **tradition**? Many of the boomers and busters who worship with us have seldom attended church since they were children going with their parents or grandparents. Many have not returned to church since their wedding days. For them, the thought of attending one of the services they remember is equivalent to anticipating a root canal. They would not attend a church that duplicates the service of their parents' churches, yet they still have a few "residual memories" of what a church must include.

Think about it. What do even non-Christians know about our faith? Most can quote John 3:16. They can get four of the ten commandments right. They can probably recite the entire Lord's Prayer and sing or hum the first verses of the top ten hymns. So we include a couple of these fixtures in our service, so that people's need to satisfy those "residual memories" will be met. Our service contains a time of prayer closed with the Lord's Prayer. We have a time for "Sharing the Word," when a family or individual reads a section out of each of the four lectionary readings. Our service usually includes at least one traditional hymn. Often our opening "Songs of Praise" are choruses, but we also use hymn medleys. Traditional stuff is woven into the service, and meets a need we all have to obtain the approval of our parents.

Don't get me wrong. I grew up with, love and find great solace in these **traditions**, but I am talking about the outlook and attitude of people who are not necessarily "church-minded."

WITH A *Twist*

Most of our members who have habitually attended church for a long time say they feel at home in our service because of the traditional points and style. On the other hand, most of our longtime unchurched people say, "This is nothing like the church my parents forced me to suffer through." How can these contradictory statements be made about the same church? It's because we do things with a *twist*!

We have changed the names of things. We give traditional events new names, and create our own modern terminology. For example, "A Call to Worship" is a chorus of invitation to God, such as "He is Here," "He is Lord," "Spirit of the Living God" and other titles such as these, with a prayer by the pastor tagged on to the end. We don't call our choruses "Praise and Worship," because that is charismatic terminology that turns this group of people off, so we came up with "Songs of Praise." We don't call our prayer time "The Pastoral Prayer," we call it "Joys and Concerns." Our Scripture reading is "Sharing the Word." The closing song is not an "Invitational Hymn" but a "Hymn of Hope." We end not with a "Benediction," but with a "Congregational Benediction" where we all share in an upbeat or uplifting sending-forth song such as "The Trees of the Field" or "On Eagles' Wings." We don't have a choir. Often choirs were the main warring faction in the old-guard churches. For many people, "the choir" carries some bad connotations, so we have a "Hope Ensemble." These are small things, but they convey a different perspective and attitude, and they fit us.

BE *Comfortable*

Most of all be *comfortable*. Be you! One of the things that most visiting pastors and church leaders say to us is that our service "fits who we are." You might be thinking, "Well, we are Methodist, Baptist, Presbyterian or whatever, and we do it this way! I am not going to change." Hey, if you will remember the downward spiraling circle we talked about earlier in which almost every mainline denomination is caught, and you want to die for a lost cause, that's okay. But remember that the captain goes down with the ship.

Do your own thing, be yourself, be *comfortable*, but do it with **FIZZ**, a little tradition, maintain some **flexibility** and add a *twist*.

PLANNING FOR YOUR FIRST SERVICE

Before we put our bread into the oven, here are three quick reminders. Just as you use good baking accessories to make great bread, you will want to put quality into your first service in the following ways.

DON'T BE CHEAP

I didn't say be expensive. I just say "don't be cheap!" when equipping the church. Enough said.

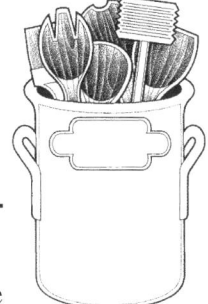

LET LEADERS LEAD

As you prepare your quadrilateral areas, be sure that the vision, mission and philosophy statements are kept in check. You should give some basic examples, but let your leadership teams set your greeting routine, children's church and nursery policies and procedures, and so forth. These people will have to do them, lead them and enforce them, and they will be more likely to believe in them if they choose them. Your nudging and counsel may be helpful, but only if it concerns life-and-death issues, or if you have not chosen the right people for the job and have not done a good job of sharing your vision with them.

Trust your leadership! You cannot run everything yourself in a fast-growing church, and you need to let your leaders make their own mistakes and learn some of their own lessons.

PREHEAT THE OVEN: DRESS REHEARSAL

Every oven is different. Gas is the best for baking because it heats the oven more evenly and responds to temperature changes more quickly, compared to the slow-reacting electric oven. Good cooks know the ins and outs of their equipment. Learn about your church equipment as well. You don't want to start your first service and then find out something doesn't work or the people can't see or hear you.

> **FOUR THINGS THAT NEED TO BE DONE IN "PREHEATING" YOUR CHURCH FOR ITS FIRST SERVICE:**
> - ☑ Set-up
> - ☑ Walk through
> - ☑ Run through
> - ☑ Think through

We held a mock service the week before our first service at Highland Hope. We went through our set-up, ran a children's church program (using kids), operated our nursery for the babies present, walked through our worship service with music so our sound system people could work out the kinks and practiced greeting visitors. We even had mock visitors. This exercise allowed us to position ourselves, try out our procedures and make a list of last-minute things to do.

While in Florida writing this book I went to eat at a local place called Pompano Joe's at 3:00 in the afternoon. In the back of the restaurant were the four owners, the chef and the manager, with lots of plates on the table. I tried to get a glimpse of what they were doing, and an owner caught my eye and invited me to come back. They were preparing sample dishes for their new 1997 menu. They invited me to taste all kinds of things—Cajun fried shrimp, pineapple chicken salad in a hulled-out pineapple and sword fish with a sauerkraut based sauce on top. What a great idea!

I think we will do the same for our service at Highland Hope annually. We will look at our service, see what's doing well and what's not. Maybe a new look here or taste there would provide a welcomed fresh insight. Even network news programs change their sets occasionally, and it's not a bad idea to do the same with our churches, ministries and services.

In September 1997 we made some changes that included ditching all but an occasional hymn, replacing the "Sharing the Word" with a "Drama Team Moment" and placing the Scripture inside the interaction of the sermon. On the third Sunday of the month, we lean toward more traditional hymns and serve Communion, and call this "Celebration Sunday—a service of Consecration and Communion." Each of these changes have been made to stay out front and on the cutting edge, and as a result more people have gotten involved in our worship services.

MAKE INTO SEVERAL LOAVES: THE EVENT!

Now you have made all this dough and have spent all this time (about seven hours). Are you just going to make one loaf? No way. I always make double or triple recipes. They don't take much longer to mix, and I can enjoy bread, give it away and have some every night for a week. At this point in developing a new church, you have spent thousands of hours discipling, training and planning with your people to get to the first service. Now, even though this first service is crucial, do not plan on your first event being it. Not everyone will come the first week, so plan the event as a month-long activity, an introductory period.

SEE THE MONTH AS THE EVENT, AN INTRODUCTION

Advent did this nicely for us. The four Sundays of Advent, thematically, are Hope, Peace, Love and Joy. Each Sunday, beginning with Hope and ending with Joy, which fell on Christmas Eve, we celebrated those aspects of God. My sermon series was entitled "The Gift," and the sermons were "A Gift of Hope," "A Gift of Peace," "A Gift of Love" and "A Gift of Joy."

PULL OUT ALL THE STOPS

Don't hold back because many people won't be back. Use your best musicians, your best singers, your best sermon. Do not save anything from this first service or hold back this entire month. Plan, work, study, do your homework, make sure that you put your very best foot forward. This is the state of the union address, in a presidential sense, and what is said, done and presented in your first service may be your one and only chance to attract some families in your inaugural month.

Don't pull your punches. Knock them out. Be honest, don't hide who you are, be real and just do it. And then maintain that level of quality in your services. It will be tough. I work hard to have a "knockout" service each week. Growing churches don't grow because of gimmicks, they grow

GROWING CHURCHES DON'T GROW BECAUSE OF GIMMICKS, THEY GROW THROUGH HARD WORK BY THEIR PASTORS AND MEMBERS.

through hard work by their pastors and members. If you get used to laying on the couch, it becomes easy. If you get used to running two miles each morning, that becomes easier. If you get used to running five miles each day, it gets easier. If you work hard, practice hard and get in shape, doing top-notch work will become easier. Excellence is habitual, and so is a lack of it. Get in shape! Too many churches are already foundering.

STAND BACK, MARVEL AND REVIEW: POST-SERVICE EVALUATION, FOLLOW-UP AND ADJUSTMENTS

Celebrate with your leaders! Celebrate with your family! Make audiotapes, videotapes and take photographs. This is a historic occasion. Your people deserve a time of excitement, well-deserved thanks, hugs and a day off. Go home and relax!

However, you should pre-plan a review session for the *following* evening to review the service and plan any adjustments or deal with any problems before next week. (Don't do this on Sunday—celebrate that day!) As you evaluate the service, let people share their experiences. Let them share the responses of their friends, family and neighbors who came. Then hear reports from each of the "Benitone Quadrilateral" areas and walk through the service.

Pastors, be sure to write personal notes of thanks to all of your leaders and service participants. Do it right away; do it for specialists each and every week. Every Monday, I pick a couple of special people and send them a note of thanks. Keep your well primed. Everyone deserves a pat on the back and an old fashioned "Atta Boy!" every now and then. *Hand write and hand address these notes yourself, no matter how bad your handwriting is*—it's good etiquette.

One last note: As you review your first service, remember to look at the project and not the people. Personal criticism does not belong in the church. Sin is our enemy, never people. Jesus died for people! He cares dearly for your people—do likewise!

STEP SIX: GLAZE WITH OLIVE OIL

PRESENTATION: ACCENTS AND DECOR ARE ESSENTIAL TO GOOD BREAD

When the bread is ready to pop in the oven, I often top it off with a nice glaze of olive oil or butter. You can add lots of things to your bread before baking—herbs, nuts, whole grains—just be creative! I call this the "presentation." Now that the church is taking shape and the first Sunday of worship is behind you, you're holding regular worship services each week and looking toward expanding your congregation. You can start by reviewing the accents and decor options that are available to you.

What do I mean? I do not consider the first service the start of a "church." Our church began in September with our first home fellowship group. However, I believe it is wise to hold off on declaring your church a formal or "official" church until you have developed a base of members prepared to enter into covenant together. Often a new business will hold its "Grand Opening" months after it opens. It was open the whole time, but waited to declare its existence to the world until it had a base of customers and some network to rely on. This is a wise approach for the church. The church begins where two or three gather in the name of our Lord, but a delayed "Grand Opening" can be a useful tool for growth, outreach and evangelism if done in a position of strength rather than expediency. The United Methodist Church requires members to join the church through a profession of the Christian faith and by committing to be in covenant with the church and each other through their prayers, presence, gifts and service. Through these disciplines the church of Jesus Christ lives and operates.

> I SIMPLY INVITED PEOPLE WITH DESIRES AND IDEAS FOR MINISTRY TO SHARE THOSE WITH ME. WE WOULD PRAY, THINK AND DEVELOP THEIR IDEAS INTO CONSTRUCTIVE MINISTRY PLANS.

So you're meeting for worship. That's great. You have a leadership base. That's great, too. But twelve disciples didn't make the church complete. Rather, the 3,000, 5,000 and the many others who have been added since have formed the body of Christ called the Church. It's not the quantity that counts, but it is the quality of the relationships that is most important. Now that you're into the service, you need to start the discipleship process over, allowing the new people to get involved, allowing them to integrate into the various ministries, finding places of their own to expand the body of Christ. This is the accents and decor.

Once we were going, I simply invited people with desires and ideas for ministry to share those with me. We would pray, think and develop their ideas into constructive ministry plans. From December 3, 1995, to now we started the following ministries:

> **Women's Bible Study**—Uses the "Experiencing God" literature. Lay initiated and led.
>
> **Pray & Play**—A Wednesday morning gathering for stay-at-home mothers and fathers. Parents pray together and let the kids play. Lay initiated and led.
>
> **Highland Hope Golfers**—A group that plays inner-church scrambles bimonthly and enters area benefit tournaments as a church team. I initiated this one, but others will be taking over in the new year. This has done wonders for our men's relationships, out of which our Men's Ministry is developing.

Men's Ministry—A Promise Keepers-based group that is forming as I write this book. Lay initiated and led.

Sunday School—Will begin this December 1 on our first anniversary. This ministry is being led by 12 lay teachers and an administrative assistant who is a lay person.

Dinner for Eight home groups, Vacation Bible School, Summer Camping, The Hope Brigade Basket Ministry, Youth Focus, and more are coming . . .

My rule of thumb is that if a ministry is valid and needed, God will provide the people, the calling, the leadership and the support to bring it together. The only ministry I have started beyond worship is the golf team. You ask, "Why?" I like golf! I have very little personal involvement beyond being an encourager and resource person in any of the ministries listed above, and that is not going to change. God is doing a great thing!

As our congregation grows, as people continue to develop in their faith and as their hearts turn toward God, the development of ministries, programs and services at Highland Hope is bound to be amazing.

Where do we go from here? I believe you need to set some goals. If you have a goal, you can reach a point that you can "Charter," "Officially Dedicate," "Enter into a Formal Covenant" or whatever your terminology is for officially declaring your church constituted. In the United Methodist tradition a church becomes an official place of worship when it is chartered, organized and named by the bishop. This includes the receiving of the first members, the official establishment of the required church offices and leadership teams and the official naming of the church by our bishop. Our goals to petition for charter were to be holding an average attendance of around 150, to have over 50 families ready to charter, to maintain this level for six months and to have a healthy financial base. On October 20, 1996 we chartered—what a day!

Now we will turn to the process I used to get to the point of our official church dedication.

This will be another big day in line with the date of your first organizational meeting (our picnic), the first home group fellowship, the first worship service, your charter or birth date, your land purchase date, the dedication of your building date, etc. These will all be days for ages to come that you can celebrate, look back to, vision forward from and use to promote and build your church. Baby boomers, busters and Xers love to celebrate special occasions (this is why Hallmark is thriving). We need hope, we need things to appreciate and we love to celebrate.

SURVEY YOUR POSSIBILITIES: REVIEW YOUR LEADERSHIP, STRENGTHS AND NEEDS

As your church is developing you will need to expand your leadership teams. You will need to establish land search teams and a land fund. Don't start the building aspect until you own the land—keep the carrot out there and the money will flow better. Besides, having too much on the plate at once will be overwhelming to even the most gung-ho congregation, especially with today's building costs.

On October 22, just two days after our official chartering was completed, we purchased 15 acres of land for $84,000 in an area near our high school and the future junior high school. An adjacent corner lot is being planned for a 300-home subdivision. On the third day after charter, we held the first meeting of our 28 person/20 family Building Task Force. It was our hope to have a building site plan in hand by March of 1997 to meet some special conference funding deadlines.

Start looking at your strengths and needs as a church. Don't forget to look into the future and begin praying that God will provide those with a calling, vision and heart to see those needs. Two things I implore you to do in this process are to accentuate the positives and avoid programs while seeking ministries.

ACCENTUATE THE POSITIVES

Don't try to do things you can't. My home church had a quilting circle, and it was a strong ministry in that church. What a great idea! But, there is no way on God's green earth that a quilting circle will work at Highland Hope right now. In the future, as we age, maybe, but this is a lost art to most of my members. Accentuate the positives of your church! We have great carpenters in our church, young people with strong backs and great hearts—so a Habit for Humanity home-building project yes, quilts no. Some make quilts, some build houses, each according to their gifts and abilities.

Accentuate the positives, the strengths, the needs and desires of those in your church to do ministry. Do not dig up ministries because they're typical or denominationally expected. Allow ministries to be created that are born from the hearts of compassionate lay persons eager to serve God today.

AVOID PROGRAMS, SEEK MINISTRIES

Do not start programs. The government has programs. The women's auxiliary has programs. The police station has programs. But churches are unique—they start ministries. A ministry is defined in my book as an act of God's Grace, Mercy, Hope and Love, which invites people to build relationships with God and each other. Programs exhaust lay people and the service recipients. However, ministries meet eternal needs and allow both giver and receiver to be ministered to. Ministries turn churches on and expand and build the body of Christ. Avoid programs, seek ministries!

GLAZE WITH EXTRA VIRGIN OLIVE OIL: USING LAY PEOPLE FOR MINISTRY

When you cook Italian, there is one kind of oil to use—Extra-Virgin Olive Oil. Why Extra-Virgin? It's the first pressing of the olives, so it's new, usable and has a great flavor. Olive oil makes the food a "true blessing" to eat. In the church the olive has a different but special heritage that reaches back to the time of Christ. Olives have served for centuries for making an oil of divine blessing. In doing church development, I encourage you to see this as an opportunity to use lay people, the olive oil of the church, to do ministry through which God can anoint and bless. It is not the oil that God blesses, but it is the faith that it is applied and the name in which it is proclaimed that gives faith the strength and power to heal and bless. Teach your people to have faith in God and to apply that faith in ministry, and your church will grow and become vibrant. Following are a few keys in this process.

USE LAY PEOPLE

Don't hire staff to start ministries. Professional staff are appropriate for secretarial, pastoral, educational and other areas that require special educational training. Staffing might be used to supervise, encourage, develop and support the laity who start ministries, but *use lay people* to run the ministries. They are the church.

FIND YOUR LAY PEOPLE BY USING TOUCH POINTS

See the ministries of your church as touch points by offering and allowing ministries to grow and develop. These touch points can provide your new members and those in your church who are seeking to fulfill a need with opportunities to spark their own callings to serve God and each other. As I talk with new families at Highland Hope, I ask them about their needs, interests and desires. I then begin to pray that they may find, develop or participate in a ministry that will help them fulfill those desires and get in touch with their spiritual giftedness, themselves and God.

PRAY FOR GOD'S ANOINTING ON THESE PEOPLE

As their pastor, your job should be to provide counsel, encouragement, direction, healing, feeding and support to your sheep—the laity. But your greatest responsibility is to share the Word of God and, I believe, hold them before God in prayer. "The prayer of the righteous is powerful and effective" (James 5:16, NRSV).

LAYPEOPLE DO MINISTRY, PASTORS SIMPLY TEND THEM

Stay out of their way. Don't feel insecure. Don't feel threatened. Don't feel lessened because your lay people are expanding and growing the ministries of your church beyond even your own vision. Many pastors choose to be like a shepherd, watching over the flock, making all the decisions for the flock. Day in and day out, the shepherd leads, guides and makes every decision for the flock. Most shepherds dream of that day when they will have the Bonanza of sheep farms, but the problem with this is that the shepherd is limited to the size of the one flock he/she can tend. I prefer what a friend calls "the Rancher Model." The rancher is still a shepherd of sheep, but forms groups of under-shepherds who tend flocks. This is typical of a lot of churches today. Pastors relate to group leaders and leaders to the group members. In this model a pastor can tend herds of flocks versus the sheep of one flock. Try the Rancher Model and you will be able to do much more.

You may still be worried, "How? How will I supervise all these ministries and people who will filter in through them if I, the pastor, am not in charge, am not there every day, at every meeting, present every time the doors to the church are open, carefully watching over the sheep and extending the only divinely chosen hand of God in the church?" You won't! If the expansion of the kingdom of God is up to you, you are living with a God-complex, and will never get anywhere.

> I PREFER WHAT A FRIEND CALLS "THE RANCHER MODEL." A RANCHER IS STILL A SHEPHERD OF SHEEP, BUT FORMS GROUPS OF UNDER-SHEPHERDS WHO TEND FLOCKS.

Follow this very carefully, pastors. How do sheep multiply? Sheep have sheep. And sheep have more sheep, and on and on. Have you ever seen a shepherd have a sheep? Of course not!—At least not yet. Let your sheep multiply, let them build the church—it's theirs. Your role should be as a spiritual midwife, helping them in their struggle. They will be there long after you're gone and, if allowed, they will do their work out of love. After all, there are a lot more sheep than pastors. As all sheep love their newborns, your people will love their sheep. You are but a hired gun. While your calling will give you the heart to love the sheep, you are still a paid, job-on-the-line, rent-a-friend. Now this doesn't exempt you from doing your own personal evangelism as a Christian. You should bear your own sheep, but you are not required to provide for the entire birth rate of the church. It is your job to fend, defend, shear, heal, watch, protect, guide, hold, bury and educate your flock. Be faithful to that task, but let the sheep have the sheep. Good discipleship, good teaching, good preaching and good prayer will make your people into productive and fruitful Christians. This is the hope of the church, this is the hope of Christ, and this is the Great Commission.

THE TASTE TEST: LET COOL AND CHARTER/SERVE

IS IT READY? FIND GROUND ZERO

You have worked hard. You have properly combined in the proper measure all the basic ingredients that alone are practically inedible. By adding the proper additives, mixing and baking, you have created a wonderful, great-smelling, heavenly result—Italian bread. This is the goal of church planting, to come to that day when all is in place. I didn't say when all is done—that day never comes. But find your "Ground Zero."[1] Ground Zero is the point at which the church becomes a living and fruitful plant, an effective, fervent, responsible, thriving and legitimate community of faith. Only you will know when this occurs. Only you will know when your church has reached Ground Zero.

Our official charter service was Highland Hope's Ground Zero. As I close this book let me leave you with a few ideas that might bring strong closure to this process of planting a church.

---

[1] I was inspired by this concept in a great book titled *The Road to Ground Zero, Finding God's Will* by Rev. Fred Bishop as told by Shane Bishop and Roger Lipe. This book is published by Treasure House. I encourage you to read it.

PREPARE TO SERVE

Don't rest on your laurels—celebrate, marvel, cry, go out for dinner, but when the dust settles and the sun comes up the next day, move on. The birth of a church is not the end, but the beginning—Ground Zero. You now bear a new responsibility. Just like the church in Acts, the established church of Jesus Christ is responsible to disciple others so they may go out and start new churches. Your task is just beginning. Baking the bread is the beginning. By taking the bread we are strengthened to serve. Even the Eucharist, the body of Christ, is a reminder to serve. Re-access your vision, review your mission, update your philosophy and "Bring forth the royal diadem."[2]

PASTOR'S CLASSES

As you prepare to charter, be sure everyone knows what they are joining. The way to do this is by having what I call a "Pastor's Class." I have held over fifteen of these to date, and am still adding classes. The class lasts four hours and can be done in one, two or four sessions. Each hour is designed to help the participants form the questions they might need in exploring their hearts and minds before becoming a covenant partner in our church. Classes are limited to 10 to 12 persons. Families are encouraged to attend together when possible, and they are all done in a small group setting with at least one or two other households represented. This was designed to be a type of confirmation class. Children in the sixth grade or under were asked to wait for our spring confirmation class, which is given for sixth graders and is more in-depth and geared to young Christians or exploring candidates.

There is lots of material out there you could use, but I did my homework and decided to write my own, which is outlined in Figure 9-1. Why? So it would better speak to the non-churched, giving them a glimpse of the Christian faith and inviting them to respond, and not simply preparing them for a ritual. Most of the other stuff I saw was designed to show the church to those already in it and was not done from a truly unchurched perspective. In some cases the material's language, examples and/or style were outdated.

---

[2] Taken from verse 1 of "All Hail the Power of Jesus' Name," No. 154 in *The United Methodist Hymnal* © 1989, The United Methodist Publishing House.

FIGURE 9-1
Pastor's Classes at Highland Hope

HOUR 1
Your Understanding of the Church and the Gifts God Has Given You

We begin with a spiritual gifts assessment. We have a time of sharing on those gifts by which we get to know each other. We then talk about our individual concepts of the church. What ministries are important and needed to have an effective church? We then review the Highland Hope vision, mission and philosophy statement. We then take questions.

HOUR 2
Foundational Christian Doctrine

We do a one-hour review of the Apostles' Creed, the Church's foundational Christian doctrine. We talk about the fact that each statement is a necessary link to building the faith. We then take questions.

HOUR 3
Wesleyan History and Theology

We spend an hour with an introduction to John Wesley and the path he took in fathering the church we call Methodist. We take a look at the theology of John Wesley in the areas of grace, salvation, sanctification, witness, outreach and others. We then take questions.

HOUR 4
United Methodist Polity and Structure

We spend the final hour going through the UM structure, organization and pastoral appointment process. We conclude with a review of the covenant of membership, exploring the language. We spend time talking about membership and what they will be becoming a part of. We conclude with questions and an invitation for them to profess their faith in Christ.

I could have required many hours of study as many new churches do, but my goal was to help people learn to formulate questions that will become a part of their spiritual formation process. The church is in it for the long term, and if the disciples couldn't get it all in three years from Jesus Christ himself, how can we expect the laity to do so in a short confirmation class?

MEMBERSHIP SURVEY

One of the things I did through the entire process, from September 1995 until September 1996, was to never pigeonhole, ask, push or coerce anyone to tell me whether they were going to be charter members of our church. We held Communion only three times in that period. The first was during the fourth Sunday of Advent, the second was for Maundy Thursday, during Holy Week, and the third was at a special service for our district superintendent. The reason I did not serve it more often was that communion in many churches is only for the privileged and has been a pawn of exclusivism for years in the church. So I waited, hoping that via the Pastor's Classes everyone would feel comfortable and Communion would not scare anyone off, but would become a special experience at Highland Hope. It has! We also performed no baptisms or any other similar services, except for one funeral. I didn't discuss stewardship or any of the things that have to do with it, and giving was excellent. Everything until September was come-as-you-are, no pressure. It was a time of getting to know one another.

Beginning in mid-September, I inquired of each participant whether or not they intended to become a charter member. I assured them that whatever decision they made would not change their relationship or value within the church, but membership was a process by which we continue to explore our relationships together. At this time I met with and had each family complete a Membership Survey. This survey included information we had, like their addresses, but also information we didn't have yet, such as dates of birth, work places, anniversaries, kids' names, middle names and interests. We also asked for previous church information, if applicable, such as baptism and other memberships, and where to send for membership transfer. They were asked to list favorite and disliked foods, special dietary concerns (this is for the home meal team which brings in meals in times of illness), any special needs, areas they previously had served in the church and whether they wanted to do it again. We entered this information into a database and used it to fill out our membership records. We then sent letters of transfer of membership to all the churches of those coming to us from other churches. These letters went all over the country. Many of these letters were sent to childhood churches from years past. We then figured out who needed to be baptized and, the week before our charter service, we held a baptismal service for all these people, borrowing the local Southern Baptist Church to do this work.

These membership surveys have been gold mines of information, and have given me a good tool to use in making our first inquiries into prospective membership. Beyond these activities, we made very few distinctions or mention of "joining the church" or "membership." We discuss it when people request it and have since planned a couple of times during the year when we intentionally invite new families to join the church if they are ready for this step. We currently have approximately 15 families that we are hoping to move toward the membership rolls in the next year, but if they don't choose to become members, they are still partners at Highland Hope.

In my situation, membership growth is expected. It is the basis by which the Conference's district superintendents evaluate the success of a new church. Regardless of this pressure, do it lightly, go easy, have a purpose, be positive and never run a family off over the desire to swell your membership rolls. Don't make growth the sole purpose of your life. Some families have really been burned by past churches. Let the scars heal, let time pass, build trust and wait on them. They will come if you build it; they will make their decision in their time, as most have and I expect most will. But try pushing a family of this generation in a direction against their will, and I guarantee they will buck back. And if by chance they don't and they go along begrudgingly, then what do you have? I doubt anyone will be dragged into heaven by twisting their arms up behind their back. Do not beg or drag people—Jesus didn't.

TIME OF REFLECTION AND CELEBRATION—CHARTER EVE DINNER

Take a time to reflect on and celebrate your accomplishments as a pastor and church. I will assure you that Highland Hope's Charter Sunday was a day of joyful tears this congregation will most likely carry forth for generations to come. We hit Ground

Zero before our very eyes. What a day! We celebrated this time by having a Charter Eve dinner banquet.

We held a catered dinner, utilizing the nearby Troy UMC's fellowship hall, and feasted in the biblical tradition. I planned no boring speaker, just a time of eating and a time of reflection. We did the reflection through a trivia game. I wrote up questions about first dates and times and events in the life of Highland Hope that we had shared together since the beginning. I then picked up prizes, gag gifts and nice gifts, and we let the question winners draw for them. We closed the evening with an invitation to let anyone share a moment of reflection on "what Highland Hope has meant to me." I'll tell you, the memories of those who spoke bring tears to my eyes now. Over and over people shared how relationships, the church and God had become a real part of their lives, and how they were excited about God and the Church. *This is a treasure coming out of the mouths of today's buster, boomer and Xer generations.* As we closed this time of reflection, there was complete agreement by all the conference leaders and Highland Launch Team members who were honored guests at the banquet that this church had become a family—a family of God.

GIVE THANKS TO GOD: CHARTER AND SERVE

I give all thanks to God for the opportunity to do the work he called me to. I give all thanks to God for the people he has allowed me to work and build new relationships with. I thank God that long after I move on to start new churches, to retire, to do whatever, he will be doing something special in a place he was not before.

I planted an oak tree when I was young, and each time I drive past my childhood home I marvel at God's gift of the huge tree that now resides there. I tear up at thinking that I was privileged to move some of God's earth, to share some of his living water, to benefit from his Son's light, and through God's love and grace to see something grow to such magnificence. I feel so insignificant in the light of God's plan and God's vision, but still what a privilege it is to be able to tend his garden a while and to make a difference.

In this book I have talked about how to "bake" a church from scratch. Now the task for me and us is to learn how to serve a church baked from scratch. Hmmm . . . that may be the inspiration for another book someday.

I hope this information, while it is not foolproof, and it is not some trick method to build your own kingdom, will show you how I, by God's grace, was able to participate in a miracle. In the light of God's Grace, Mercy and Power, I am truly insignificant, but I was privileged to still be a part of the miracle of Highland Hope.

> **Praise God, from whom all blessings flow;**
> **Praise him, all creatures here below;**
> **Praise him above, ye heavenly host;**
> **Praise Father, Son, and Holy Ghost.**
> **Amen!**[3]

THE END

No Way. It's just the beginning!

HIGHLAND HOPE UNITED METHODIST CHURCH

~

CHARTERED OCTOBER 20, 1996

---

[3] "Praise God, from Whom All Blessings Flow," No. 95 in *The United Methodist Hymnal,* © 1989, The United Methodist Publishing House. This hymn is often used as a doxology.

HINTS: APPENDIX

SOME TIPS FROM THE CHEF

1. A Brief Framework for Starting New Congregations
2. Sample "Looking for Hope?" Brochure
3. Sample Invitations to Various Events
4. Sample Newspaper Ads
5. Sample Office and Worship Setup Equipment Lists
6. Operating Expense Budget 1996 and 1997
7. Highland Hope's Time Line
8. Leadership Qualities Needed for New Start Pastors
9. Mentor Church Program
10. Sample SS-4 Application for FEIN (Federal Employer Number)
11. A Copy of Our Actual FEIN Form
12. Sample 501(c)3 IRS Letter for Tax Exemption
13. Sample Worship Bulletin
14. Recipe for Classic Italian Bread

1. A BRIEF FRAMEWORK FOR STARTING NEW CONGREGATIONS

Step 1: Prayer
How we hear the voice of God.

Step 2: Calling to the task
Finding leadership called to this task.

Step 3: Perspective
Christianity is a demonstration sport and not a spectator sport. Effective new churches will engage and involve people and will become-ministry focused and people-focused rather than ego-driven and self-centered.

Step 4: Plan for Starting a New Service or Congregation
Create a vision and mission statement, then be flexible. If I could tell you how far Highland Hope has journeyed from my preconceived plan and picture, but how much greater it has become through the power of the body of Christ, you would be amazed.

Step 5: Target Group and Location
Select a target group—intentionality is the key to success. Learn your target group and locations:

Sociological background—ages, children, child-bearing statistics, educational levels, job makeup (white collar, blue collar, industrial, agricultural, etc.)

Economic background—Average income, median household worth, average home values, property value growth over the last 5–10–20 years and projected inflation rate over the next 1–5–10 years.

Ecumenical background—What are existing churches doing, what is the average church attendance for the town, how does that break down per church, does one church have a predominance? Look at the average age of existing congregations. Are they growing, static or shrinking? Review their ministries and what is successful.

Step 6: Create a Target Family
Who are they?

Step 7: Create a Philosophy of Ministry
Use your vision and mission statement along with the philosophy of ministry. Any philosophy that does not include community involvement, family ministries, new residential evangelization and the presentation of a Gospel of Hope will find itself quickly rejected and ineffective to many of the boomers, busters and Xers.

Step 8: Metholodogy
Plan and think ahead of the developmental phases you will go through. Plan some milestones to measure your growth and effectiveness at different levels. This is part of study and effective planning, however, be prepared to react and be flexible if the Holy Spirit leads differently. Even in an early stage you want to be intentional, developing and watching for the leadership needed for future stages—this requires knowing where you're going. Yes, Moses wandered in the desert for 40 years, but he did know where he was going.

The phases of Highland Hope were:

1. The parsonage, settling in and covert operation phase.
2. Developing an accountability and oversight team.
3. Introductory phase—Prospect lists, promotion, brochure campaign, home phoning campaign, etc.
4. Home fellowship phase—Beginning small groups.
5. Leadership development phase.
6. Worship phase.
7. Congregational development phase.
8. Charter phase/reception of first members.
9. Land and building phase.

Step 9: Spirit-Led, Prayer-Bathed, Heart-Led execution of Steps 1–8
If there is any doubt or failure stop and repeat Step 1.

2. SAMPLE "LOOKING FOR HOPE?" BROCHURE

Looking for Hope?

Highland HOPE

"Have an Answer for the Hope!"
1 Peter 3:15

A developing Congregation of the United Methodist Church

Highland Hope
23 Triland Ct.
Highland, IL 62249

First Class Stamp

Directions to Highland Hope:
1 4/10 miles west from the intersection of Rt. 40 and Walnut St./Rt. 143 (Bonanza is at this intersection)

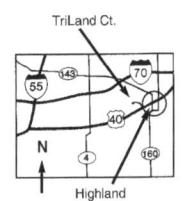

Call (618) 654-8434 for further directions.

Highland Hope
c/o Rev. Troy D. Benitone
23 Triland Ct.
Highland, IL 62249

Appendix

What is Highland Hope?

Highland Hope is a vision. A vision of a new church congregation designed to meet the spiritual needs of you and your family!

HIGHLAND HOPE IS:

A NEW DEVELOPING CONGREGATION.

A PLACE TO GROW SPIRITUALLY.

AN OPPORTUNITY FOR INVOLVEMENT IN A NEW CHRISTIAN FELLOWSHIP.

Who is Highland Hope For?

Highland Hope is for people just like you. People with hopes and dreams. People who want to better learn to love God and each other.

HIGHLAND HOPE IS FOR:

PEOPLE LOOKING FOR A CHURCH HOME.

PEOPLE WHO WANT A CHURCH THAT IS EXCITING AND FUN.

PEOPLE OF ALL AGES AND STAGES.

Meet the Pastor

Rev. Troy D. Benitone is the Pastor of Highland Hope. He is an ordained minister in the United Methodist Church, and has a Masters of Divinity degree from Emory University. Rev. Troy, along with his wife Beth, daughter Heather, and two sons, Joshua and Caleb, have been assigned to the Highland Community.

How Can I Be A Part?

Highland Hope is about people, not a building. You can become a part by returning the attached postcard or calling us for additional information.

HIGHLAND HOPE IS IN NEED OF:

PEOPLE WHO WANT TO BE A PART OF SOMETHING NEW.

PEOPLE WHO WANT TO CREATE A CHURCH TO MEET TODAY'S NEEDS.

PEOPLE WHO WANT TO LOVE GOD WITH ALL OF THEIR HEART, MIND, SOUL & STRENGTH.

If you would be interested in finding out more about Highland Hope or how you can become a part of one of our home fellowships, please feel free to call or return this self-addressed card with the following information:

Last Name: _____ First Name: _____

Address: _____

City: _____ State: _____ Zip: _____

Phone: _____

What is a good time for us to call and set up an appointment?
    Day of Week: _____ Time of Day: _____

For more information on how to be a part of Highland Hope call or write Rev. Troy Benitone at:

Highland Hope
23 Triland Ct.
Highland, IL 62249
Phone: (618) 654-8434

3. SAMPLE INVITATIONS TO VARIOUS EVENTS

This helpful map was included in all invitations.

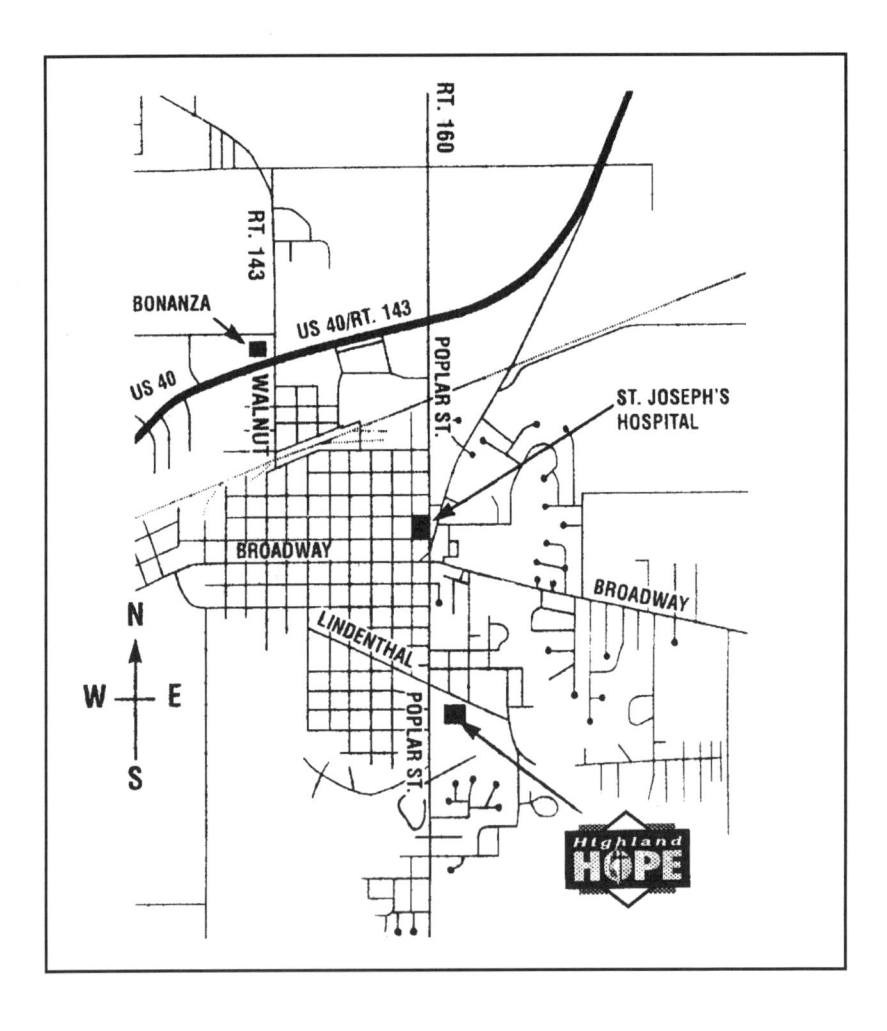

You are cordially invited to the
Charter Worship Service
of a new congregation
of the United Methodist Church

Highland HOPE

Sunday, October 20, 1996

Continental Breakfast served with
Bishop Sharon Brown Christopher
at 9:30 a.m.

Charter Worship Service
at 10:30 a.m.

Highland Middle School Auditorium
at 1800 Lindenthal

A nursery will be provided.

3. SAMPLE INVITATIONS (CONTINUED)

*You are invited
to celebrate a new beginning
as*

Highland HOPE

*holds its first worship service
Sunday, December 3, 1995
10:30 a.m.*

*Highland Middle School Auditorium
at 1800 Lindenthal*

∾

*Highland Hope is a Developing Congregation of
the United Methodist Church*

A Nursery & Children's Church will be provided.

∾

For more information, call 654-8434

Highland Hope UMC Welcomes you to come to their Worship Services

Date:

Place:

Time:

Mar. 23, Palm Sunday Open House
Highland Middle Schl. Auditorium
1800 Lindenthal Ave.
10:30 a.m.

A professionally staffed Nursery & Children's Church is available.

Highland Hope UMC offers something for everyone

*Christian Education Ministry
*Men's Ministries
*Women's Ministries
*Youth Ministry
*Kid's Kingdom Ministry
*Puppet Ministry

*And much, much, more . . . .

3. SAMPLE INVITATIONS (CONTINUED)

You Are Cordially Invited to a Special

"Friends of Hope Sunday"
Sunday, May 19

9:45 a.m. Continental Breakfast and Open House
10:25 a.m. Worship Service
at

Highland Hope United Methodist Church
Worship location:
Highland Middle School Auditorium
1800 Lindenthal Ave., Highland, IL.
&
Church Office:
23 Triland Ct., Highland, IL. 654-8434

"A professionally staffed nursery & children's church is available."

4. SAMPLE NEWSPAPER ADS

Looking for Hope?

Highland HOPE

"Have an Answer for the Hope!"
1 Peter 3:15

Beginning Worship Services
December 3rd, 1995
10:30 a.m.
at the
Highland Middle School Auditorium
at 1800 Lindenthal Ave.
For More Information please call
the church office at 654-8434.

A developing Congregation of the United Methodist Church

4. SAMPLE NEWSPAPER ADS
(CONTINUED)

*Celebrate the Birth of Christ
at Highland Hope UMC's
Special Christmas Worship Service:*
"A Blending of Traditions"

Highland HOPE

*December 22, 1995
at 10:30 a.m.*

*Highland Middle School Auditorium
1800 Lindenthal Avenue*

A professionally staffed nursery is available.

*For more information, please contact
the Church Office @ 654-8434.*

Highland HOPE

"Have an Answer for the Hope!"
1 Peter 3:15

HIGHLAND HOPE IS:

A New developing congregation

•

A Place to grow spiritually

•

An opportunity for involvement in a new Christian fellowship.

HIGHLAND HOPE IS FOR:

People looking for a church home

•

People who want a church that is exciting and fun

•

People of all ages and stages

HIGHLAND HOPE IS IN NEED OF:

People who want to be a part of something new.

•

People who want to create a church to meet today's needs

•

People who want to love God with all of their heart, mind, soul & strength.

**Beginning Worship Services
December 3rd, 1995
10:30 a.m.
at the
Highland Middle School Auditorium
at 1800 Lindenthal Avenue.**

For more information please call the church office at 654-8434.

A Developing Congregation of the United Methodist Church.

4. SAMPLE NEWSPAPER ADS
(CONTINUED)

Highland Hope

Cordially invites You to a Special "Friends of Hope Sunday"
Sunday, May 19

9:45 a.m. Continental Breakfast and Open House
10:25 a.m. Worship Service
at
Highland Hope United Methodist Church
Worship location:
Highland Middle School Auditorium
1800 Lindenthal Ave., Highland, IL

❧

Church Office
23 Triland Ct., Highland, IL 654-8434
"A professionally staffed nursery & children's church is available"

Highland Hope United Methodist Church

Church Ofc: 23 Triland Ct., Ph. 654-8434

Sunday Worship at the Highland Middle School

Auditorium at 1800 Lindenthal • Sunday Worship Time: 9:25 am

A Nursery and Children's Church is available

Highland Hope has enjoyed the great atmosphere and community of Highland. Highland Hope currently has over 70+ active families and an average worship attendance from 130–150. We are looking forward to an exciting year as we enter into our second year. As a new forming United Methodist Church we have a family focus supported by a progressively traditional worship service that is biblically based and supported with a strong music ministry and many opportunities to get involved in small groups and ministries. If you're not actively involved in a local church or have just moved to the Highland Community, Highland Hope is the place for you with a majority of our people in their 20–40s and having moved to Highland in the last 8 years. If you would be interested in further information on our Church, ministries or worship service please feel free to contact Rev. Troy Benitone, the pastor.

5. SAMPLE OFFICE AND WORSHIP SETUP EQUIPMENT LISTS

Item		Purchaser	Budget	Spent	Balance
WORSHIP EQUIPMENT (Those w/astrick have been pd.)					
Cargo Trailer		Larry's	4000	-3994 *	
Sub-total			4000	-3994	6
Nursery Equipment			2000		
Walmart equipment		St.Mat		-1130.35 *	
Child Church Equip-Kgdom,Sams		Troy		-164.73 *	
Toys R'US		Terri		-99.66	
Nursery Kraft supplies		Terri		-140	
Nursery/Child Church smocks		Silkworm		-68.27	
Sub-total			2000	-1603.01	396.99
Children's Church Equipment			500		
Tables and Chairs	S/H+126.80	Hertz		-703.1	
Sub-total			500	-703.1	-203.1
Sound System			2500		
Audio Centrion 12 channel sys		Phelps		-2400 *	
Mics, cords, speakers, tape deck, etc.					
Sub-total			2500	-2400	100
Chancel Pulpit & Altar			2200		
Pulpit		Prestige		-1800 *	
Altar Shipping		Prestige		-150	
Counters for Nursery, Sd Sys, Grters- Equip for co		Aviston Lum		-503.54	
Sub-total			2200	-2453.54	-253.54
Other Misc Chanel Items			500		
Bill for Casters for Pulpit & Altar containers		Bryan Smith		-100.6	
Bill for Wheels, stain and misc for 3 counters		Terri		-100.44	
Silk Tree- Plants and Misc candles and decor		Terri		-227.5	
Kgdm Treasures Candles for Altar & Advent		Terri		-32.87	
Worship equip purchased at Sam's		Troy		-208.51	
Sub-total			500	-669.92	-169.92
TOTAL BUDGETED- SPENT- BALANCE LEFT			15000	15123.57	-123.57

Keith according to my figures this runs over our $15,000 allowment, so I would assume some portion of the new expenses new to be paid throught Highland Account.

The Shipping Charges on the Church Furniture was $126.80 a bit more than I estimated.

Appendix

Setup Expense Report
August 14th, 1995

Requested and Approved by Board of Global Ministries for setup: $ 2550.00

(To be used to purchase office equipment to setup Highland. Items to include: copier, laser printer, fax, office furniture & equipment.)

Items Purchased: (NYP = Not Yet Purchased/ WNP = Will Not Purchase)

1. Copier – Xerox #5310 (w/1 Year Service Contract)
   EST Cost per unit – $899.99 (Office Depot Price) $ 686.48

2. Xerox Toner – #6R359 (Good for approx. #12,000 copies)
   EST Cost per unit – $110.00 (req. *2 Units) $ 188.97

3. Xerox Drum – #13R55 (Good for approx. #12,000 copies)
   EST Cost per unit – $135.00 (req. 1 unit) $ WNP

4. Sharp Fax UX-254 (Fax, Digital Answering Machine, Cutter)
   EST Cost per unit – $250.00 $ 234.98

5. Okidata Laser Printer (2mb, 4ppm, 600dpi)
   EST Cost: $500 (HP Laser Jet 4L/Epson 1500
   1mb, 4ppm, 300dpi) $ 404.99

6. ITT Phone System (4 line/4 phone/Intercom/Speaker phone)
   EST Cost – $399.00 $ 359.99

7. High Back Desk Chair – Black $ 141.98

8. Modular-Copier file organizer $ 68.99

9. GTE Business Installation Cost ($150 appropriated/
   Cost $334.46) $ 334.46

10. Table – Globe 60' Round table (Sam's $69.99) $ 78.97

11. Chairs – #8 Chrome/Blue Padded chairs $19.99
    (Sam's – $159.62) $ 176.64

Total of Items Purchased as of August 14th   **$ 2676.28**
   Overage covered through general budget

(For Inventory Purposes items #2, #3 and #9 are consumable.)

6. OPERATING EXPENSE BUDGET 1996 AND 1997

Operating Budget		Total Annual	Total Semi-An
Highland Hope Operating Budget funded by the Conference			
Project Started July 1st 1995. Same Budget Ran for July-Dec '95 and '96			
Project Developed Local Budget in 1997			
		July 95- June 96	July-Dec 96
Initial Funding:		$50,000.00	$26,000.00
Set-up Expenses:		$2,550.00	$2,550.00
*Add. Fdg for School Cong Developmt per Jim Rhea's 8/2/95 ltr		$600.00	
*Add. Fdg approved for Brochure per Jim's 8/10 ltr		$2,140.00	
*MOVING EXPENSE REIMBURSEMENT		$1,500.00	
*Request for Increase in budget (See note at bottom)		$1,192.96	
*Local Churches/Adanced Special (As of 12/31 report)		$7,117.65	$1,886.16
Total Funding to date		$65,100.61	$30,436.16
Pastoral Support:			
Pastoral Salary	($25,000.00)		($13,250.00)
Housing Allowance Paid By Conference	($8,000.00)		($4,000.00)
Pensions	($5,714.00)		($2,857.00)
Health Insurance Prem	($5,244.00)		($2,622.00)
Total Pastoral Support		($43,958.00)	($22,729.00)
Phone Bill	($870.00)		($435.00)
Utilities (1050t/2350ft=45% Base =$1500))	($675.00)		($337.00)
Total Facilities Expense		($1,545.00)	($772.00)
Reimbursable Accounts:			
Travel Reimbursement	($1,500.00)		($750.00)
One time travel for Oct-School of Cong Development	($600.00)		
REQUESTED H-Hope Promo & Resrch travel	($500.00)		($500.00)
Continuing Education- Includes Ann Conf	($400.00)		($200.00)
Total Reimbursable Accounts		($3,000.00)	($1,450.00)
Office Expense:			
Postage: (Orig 990 an/req Inc $262.40 =$1252.40)	($1,252.40)		($626.20)
Stationary: Business Cards,Ltr Head, Envelopes	($350.00)		($175.00)
Misc office supplies	($500.00)		($250.00)
Small Group Lit/Christian Education	($500.00)		($250.00)
Worship Supplies	($250.00)		($125.00)
Entertmt & Misc	($500.00)		($250.00)
Administrative Assistant (hired September 1996)			($6,500.00)
Moving Expense	($1,500.00)		($1,500.00)
Set-up Exp ($2,550 +126.45=2676.45)	($2,676.45)		($2,676.45)
Promotional Brochure Cost	($2,140.00)		($2,140.00)
School Rental Beginning in December 1995. $150 per wk.	($4,650.00)		($3,900.00)
(First =31 weeks/ June-Dec 96 =26 weeks)			
Total Office Expense		($13,066.45)	($18,392.65)
Total Pastoral, Facilities, Reimbursable and Office Expenses		($61,569.45)	($43,343.65)
Total Annual Funding - Total Expenses		$65,100.61	$30,436.16
Total Balance		$3,531.16	($12,907.49)
1996 Deficit was covered by local offering, which also went			
to the building fund to purchase our land site.	(Approx)	$34,000	$30,000

Appendix

Highland Hope Operating Budget

		Jan-Jun 1997		Jul-Dec 1997	
Initial Funding:			$26,000.00		$17,334.00
	*Local Churches/Advancd Special		$0.00		$0.00
	Total Funding todate		$26,000.00		$17,334.00
Pastoral Support Expenses:					
	Pastoral Salary	($16,000.00)		($16,000.00)	
	Housing Allowance	($5,500.00)		($5,500.00)	
	Pensions ($77.50 per month)	($465.00)		($465.00)	
	Health Insurance Plan	($2,622.00)	($24,587.00)	($2,622.00)	($24,587.00)
Reimbursable Expenses:					
	Utilities (1050ft/2350ft=45% base)	($500.00)		($500.00)	
	Travel, Meals & Misc Reimbursements	($750.00)		($750.00)	
	Continuing Education-Includes Ann Conf	($250.00)	($1,500.00)	($250.00)	($1,500.00)
Administrative Assistants Salary					
	28 hours per week= $280	($7,280.00)		($7,280.00)	
	Taxes	($655.20)	($7,935.20)	($655.20)	($7,935.20)
Land & Rental					
	$140 per week	($3,640.00)		($3,640.00)	
	$183 per month	($1,098.00)	($4,738.00)	($1,098.00)	($4,738.00)
Insurance					
	Liability, Property & Work Comp	($300.00)	($300.00)	($300.00)	($300.00)
NURSERY					
	Nursery (*2 works $20 each + $10 Sun Sch)	($1,300.00)	($1,300.00)	($1,300.00)	($1,300.00)
Ministries, Programs & Services:					
	Children's Church	($100.00)		($100.00)	
	Trips & Activites	($50.00)		($50.00)	
	Sunday School	($500.00)		($500.00)	
	Fellowship Breakfasts	($50.00)		($50.00)	
	Holy Week (Maundy Thur, Palm Sun, Easter)	($100.00)		($100.00)	
	Seasonal Flowers & arrangements	($50.00)		($50.00)	
	Special Promos (Open hse, frds of Hope)	($250.00)		($250.00)	
	Mother's Day	($25.00)		($25.00)	
	Father's Day	($25.00)		($25.00)	
	Graduation Sunday (8th & 12th Graders)	($100.00)		($100.00)	
	Hall of Hope Sunday/Summer Picnic	($200.00)		($200.00)	
	Summer Camping	($100.00)		($100.00)	
	Vacation Bible School	($200.00)		($200.00)	
	Misc (other special events, Music, etc..)	($250.00)	($1,900.00)	($250.00)	($1,900.00)
Missions:					
	Sports teams sponsorship	($100.00)		($100.00)	
	Discretionary Fund	($100.00)		($100.00)	
	Ministerial Association	($40.00)		($40.00)	
	Conference Apportionments	($400.00)	($640.00)	($400.00)	($640.00)
EVANGELISM:					
	Hope Brigade: (new resident baskets)	($700.00)	($700.00)	($700.00)	($700.00)
Offices Expenses:					
	Office Supplies	($300.00)		($300.00)	
	Copier Supplies	($750.00)		($750.00)	
	Phone ($150 per month)	($900.00)		($900.00)	
	Postage Fees	($600.00)		($600.00)	
	Printing Supplies	($400.00)	($2,950.00)	($400.00)	($2,950.00)
	Total Excess or Shortage:		($20,550.20)		($29,216.20)
Total Conference Support			$26,000.00		$17,334.00
Total Local Support Needed			($20,550.20)		($29,216.20)
Total Local Expenses			($46,550.20)		($46,550.20)
Total Local Support Needed			($20,550.20)		($29,216.20)
Total Funding Needed Per month:			($3,425.03)		($4,869.37)
Total Funding Needed Per week			($790.39)		($1,123.70)

Making a Church from Scratch

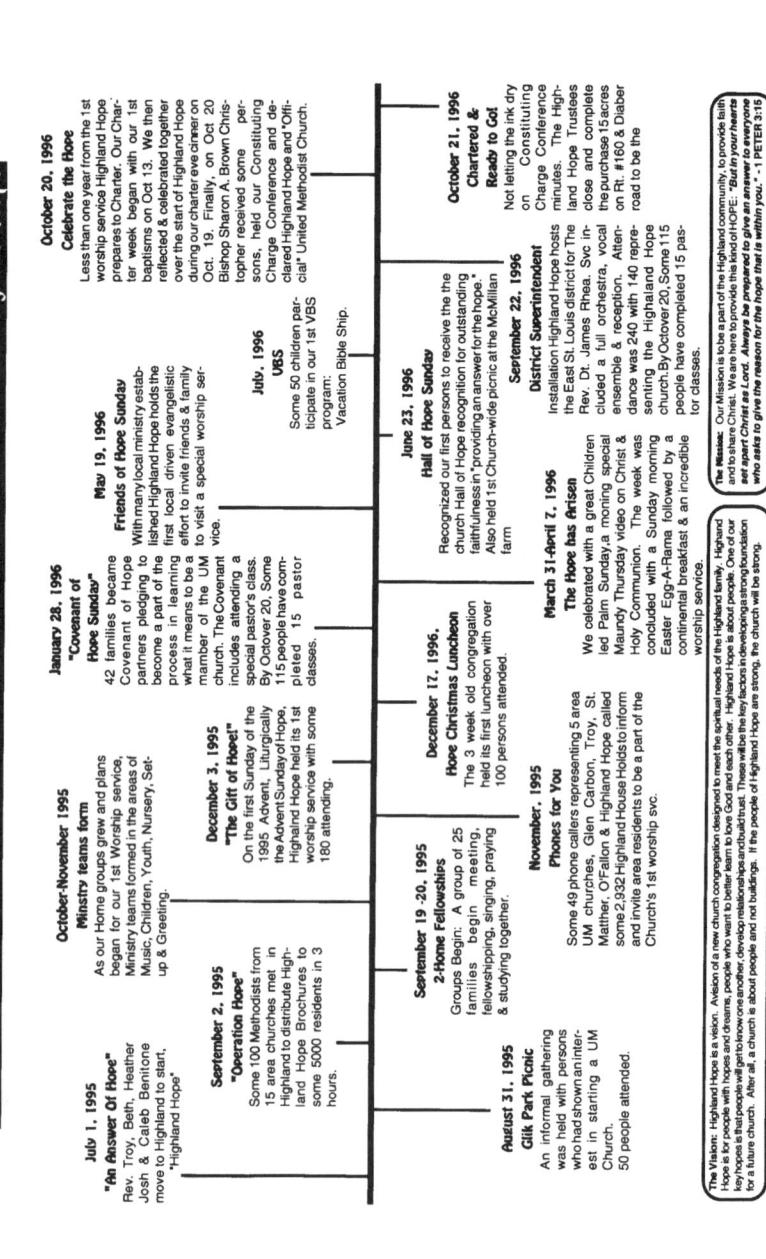

7. HIGHLAND HOPE'S TIME LINE

HIGHLAND HOPE UNITED METHODIST CHURCH: Celebrating the Hope

July 1, 1995 — "An Answer Of Hope"
Rev. Troy, Beth, Heather Josh & Caleb Benitone move to Highland to start, "Highland Hope".

September 2, 1995 — "Operation Hope"
Some 100 Methodists from 15 area churches met in Highland to distribute Highland Hope Brochures to some 5000 residents in 3 hours.

August 31, 1995 — Glik Park Picnic
An informal gathering was held with persons who had shown an interest in starting a UM Church. 50 people attended.

September 19-20, 1995 — 2-Home Fellowships
Groups Begin: A group of 25 families begin meeting, fellowshipping, singing, praying & studying together.

October-November 1995 — Ministry teams form
As our Home groups grew and plans began for our 1st Worship service, Ministry teams formed in the areas of Music, Children, Youth, Nursery, Set-up & Greeting.

November, 1995 — Phones for You
Some 49 phone callers representing 5 area UM churches, Glen Carbon, Troy, St. Matther, O'Fallon & Highland Hope called some 2,932 Highland House Holds to inform and invite area residents to be a part of the Church's 1st worship svc.

December 3, 1995 — "The Gift of Hope!"
On the first Sunday of the 1995 Advent, Liturgically the Advent Sunday of Hope, Highland Hope held its 1st worship service with some 180 attending.

December 17, 1996, Hope Christmas Luncheon
The 3 week old congregation held its first luncheon with over 100 persons attended.

January 28, 1996 — "Covenant of Hope Sunday"
42 families became Covenant of Hope partners pledging to become a part of the process in learning what it means to be a member of the UM church. The Covenant includes attending a special pastor's class. By October 20, Some 115 people have completed 15 pastor classes.

May 19, 1996 — Friends of Hope Sunday
With many local ministry established Highland Hope holds the first local driven evangelistic effort to invite friends & family to visit a special worship service.

July, 1996 — VBS
Some 50 children participate in our 1st VBS program; Vacation Bible Ship.

March 31-April 7, 1996 — The Hope has Arisen
We celebrated with a great Children led Palm Sunday, a moning special Maundy Thursday video on Christ & Holy Communion. The week was concluded with a Sunday morning Easter Egg-A-Rama followed by a continental breakfast & an incredible worship service.

June 23, 1996 — Hall of Hope Sunday
Recognized our first persons to receive the the church Hall of Hope recognition for outstanding faithfulness in "providing an answer for the hope." Also held 1st Church-wide picnic at the McMillan farm

September 22, 1996 — District Superintendent
Installation Highland Hope hosts the East St. Louis district for The Rev. Dr. James Rhea. Svc included a full orchestra, vocal ensemble & reception. Attendance was 240 with 140 representing the Highland Hope church. By October 20, Some 115 people have completed 15 pastor classes.

October 20, 1996 — Celebrate the Hope
Less than one year from the 1st worship service Highland Hope prepares to Charter. Our Charter week began with our 1st baptisms on Oct 13. We then reflected & celebrated together over the start of Highland Hope during our charter eve dinner on Oct. 19. Finally, on Oct 20 Bishop Sharon A. Brown Christopher received some persons, held our Constituting Charge Conference and declared Highland Hope and "Official" United Methodist Church.

October 21, 1996 — Chartered & Ready to Go!
Not letting the ink dry on Constituting Charge Conference minutes. The Highland Hope Trustees close and complete the purchase 15 acres on Rt. #160 & Diaber road to be the

The Mission: Our Mission is to be a part of the Highland family, Highland and to share Christ. We aim here to provide this kind of HOPE: *"But in your hearts set apart Christ as Lord. Always be prepared to give an answer to everyone who asks to give the reason for the hope that is within you." - 1 PETER 3:15*

The Vision: Highland Hope is a vision. A vision of a new church congregation designed to meet the spiritual needs of the Highland community. Highland Hope is for people with hopes and dreams, people who want to better learn to love God and each other. Highland Hope is about people. One of our key hopes is that people will get to know one another, develop relationships and build trust. These will be the key factors in developing a foundation for a future church. After all, a church is about people and not buildings. If the people of Highland Hope are strong, the church will be strong.

8. LEADERSHIP QUALITIES NEEDED FOR NEW START PASTORS

In my reading of other books regarding new church development I ran across three different lists describing the gifts a pastor needs to be equipped to work in the area of new church development. While none of these lists implied that any pastor would be perfect in all of these areas or meet all the characteristics, they did imply that the pastor should be proficient in most of these areas in order to be effective in doing the work of church planting. I pass these on to you because they are good, and they are what I used to confirm my desire to be a church planter. Before I share from these three texts, let me point out what I consider to be the top five:

1. Calling by God.
2. Support of a Christian family.
3. The vision to see the finish line before you ever arrive.
4. Confidence in God and your gifts.
5. A spirited heart.

WHAT MAKES A LEADER A LEADER?
Romans 12:8

1. Leaders have the ability to cast a vision.
2. Leaders have the ability to coalesce people.
3. Leaders have the ability to inspire and motivate people.
4. Leaders are able to identify the need for positive change—and then bring it about.
5. Leaders establish core values.
6. Leaders allocate resources effectively.
7. Leaders have the ability to identify entropy.
8. Leaders have to create a leadership culture.

From Hybels & Hybels, *Rediscovering Church,* Michigan: Zondervan Publishing House, 1995 (Chapter 9, p. 149).

8. LEADERSHIP QUALITIES NEEDED FOR NEW START PASTORS (CONTINUED)

CHARACTERISTICS OF A NEW CHURCH START PASTOR

1. A visionary
2. Spiritually centered
3. Entrepreneurial
4. Friendly, outgoing and should have a sense of humor
5. Energetic
6. A strong administrator
7. Optimistic and persistent
8. Good communicator
9. Self-confident
10. Healthy and is well matched to the community

From Stephen C. Compton & G. Steven Sallee, *Growing New Churches*, Nashville: Discipleship Resources, 19XX (Chapter 2, p. 21)

QUALIFICATIONS FOR A CHURCH PLANTER

1. Natural Qualifications
   a. Socially and educationally acceptable to the people to be reached
   b. An outgoing personality
   c. Serious, sincerely interested in people with deep concern for their personal problems
   d. Ability in public speaking
   e. An attractive personality
   f. Exemplary family life

2. Spiritual Qualifications
   a. A heart given totally to God
   b. A deep and abiding compassion for the lost

c. A life of continual prayer
   d. A life utterly dedicated to the work of the ministry
   e. A highly motivated vision

3. Attitude toward Self
   a. Certainty of God's call
   b. Honesty: confidence in God and willingness to learn
   c. Responsibility

4. Attitude toward the New Nucleus of Believers
   a. Acceptance toward those who have defects
   b. Openness toward those who have positive gifts he may not have
   c. Spiritual determination
   d. Patience, understanding, love

5. Attitude toward the Community
   a. Positive attitude
   b. Anticipation
   c. Friendliness
   d. Acceptance

From Samuel D. Faircloth, *Church Planting for Reproduction,* Michigan: Baker Book House, 1991 (Figure 10, p. 50).

9. MENTOR CHURCH PROGRAM

Highland HOPE

I. What is a Highland Hope Mentor?

> "It is a fellow United Methodist Church that has covenanted with Highland Hope to become an extended family."

II. What is the basis of the Mentor program?

The process of NEW CHURCH DEVELOPMENT is much like the baptism of an infant. As an infant the child is not able to understand, respond or be aware of the process of baptism, but regardless, through covenant with God and his people, the child becomes a part of the Christian community. We have no assurance that the child will accept that covenant at the age of accountability, but we pray that grace and our covenant will assist the child to that day of decision. In the same way we are not assured that Highland Hope will become a chartered UMC, but we pray that grace and our covenant will see that day.

III. An illustration of the covenant in infant baptisms:

The mentor acts much like the congregant as in the BAPTISMAL COVENANT II in the *United Methodist Hymnal*, pages 39–43, when they pledge to support a newly baptized infant.

༾

As Congregants/Mentors we covenant through a profession of our faith under Section 8, page 40, that we will be advocates, mentors and intercessors to the infant:

Pastor:
Will you nurture one another in the Christian faith and life and include these persons now before you in your care?

Congregational response:
With God's help we will proclaim the good news and live according to the example of Christ. We will surround these persons with

a community of love and forgiveness, that they may grow in their service to others. We will pray for them, that they may be true disciples who walk in the way that leads to life.

Finally in Section 16, page 43, we are charged in our Commendation by the pastor to remain faithful to our statement of faith:

Pastor:
Members of the household of God, I commend these persons to your love and care. Do all in your power to increase their faith, confirm their hope, and perfect them in love.

Congregational response:
We give thanks for all that God has already given you and we welcome you in Christian love. As members together with you in the body of Christ and in this congregation of The United Methodist Church, we renew our covenant faithfully to participate in the ministries of the church by our prayers, our presence, our gifts, and our service, that in everything God may be glorified through Jesus Christ.

∾

IV. Our hope for the Highland Hope Mentor Program are listed in the following main goals:
1. We are seeking a family of churches to adopt us during our spiritual journey. This should include two God Parents and two Siblings.
2. We are looking for churches far enough removed from our community not to be affected by our church's development.
3. We are asking the church to covenant with us using an edited form of the above covenant and charge.

Covenant of Faith

Pastor (to the covenanting mentor):
Will you covenant to nurture Highland Hope and its members in the Christian faith and life and include this New Church Development before you enter into your care?

Congregational response:
With God's help we will proclaim the good news and live according to the example of Christ. We will surround this New Church Development called Highland Hope with a community of love and forgiveness, that they may grow in their service to each other

9. MENTOR CHURCH PROGRAM (CONTINUED)

and to the Highland community. We will pray for them, that they may become a true lighthouse and a witness for Jesus Christ and that they might always walk with the grace and within the will of God.

Commendation and Charge

Pastor:
Members of the household of God, I commend Highland Hope to your love and care. Do all in your power to increase her faith, confirm her hope and perfect her in love.

Congregational response:
We give thanks for all that God has already begun in Highland and we welcome you in Christian love. As members together with you in the body of Christ and with our connection called The United Methodist Church, we covenant to become mentors, advocates and intercessors who will faithfully participate in the development of this new congregation by our prayers, our presence, our gifts, and our service, that in everything God may be glorified through Jesus Christ.

4. We are asking these churches to do this in a worship service, by the use of some symbol (i.e., a rose at the altar). In addition, mentor churches are to keep the congregants informed on the process of Highland's growth and make them a part of the pastoral prayer on a regular basis.
5. We are asking these churches to be advocates, mentors and intercessors.
6. We are asking these churches to make their regular worship services available to our home fellowships as they are in their formation stages. (As Home Fellowship groups/cell groups develop I plan to bring these groups to worship with these congregations. This will provide a noncompetitive insight into different settings, buildings, and worship styles as the new group seeks its own identity.)
7. We are asking these churches to covenant to assist us by providing professional consultation and assistance in preparing for our

own worship service and to be a part of and/or be represented at our first official corporate worship service in Highland.
8. We will covenant to be faithful in sharing our progress on a regular basis. We will also visit and be available to mentor churches and their organizations as they may desire.

V. Who are the Highland Mentors?

As I have spent time in prayer and reflection, I feel that many churches will be special to us, but that the following churches have some special gifts to assist this congregation in its development. I feel strongly that these churches will be important, as some have already proven, to the spiritual development of Highland Hope and as supporters of me and my family in this missionary role.

The following churches have consented to enter into this covenantal relationship:

God Parents:	St. Matthew United Methodist Church (Belleville)
	Aldersgate United Methodist Church (Marion)
Sister Church:	Sumner & Beulah United Methodist Churches
Brother Church:	O'Fallon United Methodist Church

10. SAMPLE SS-4 APPLICATION FOR FEIN (FEDERAL EMPLOYER NUMBER)

Appendix

11. A COPY OF OUR ACTUAL FEIN FORM

```
DEPARTMENT OF THE TREASURY          DATE OF THIS NOTICE:  09-28-95
INTERNAL REVENUE SERVICE            NUMBER OF THIS NOTICE:  CP 575 E
KANSAS CITY  MO    64999            EMPLOYER IDENTIFICATION NUMBER:  37-1347190
                                    FORM:  SS-4
                                    0916504651  0


                                                    FOR ASSISTANCE CALL US AT:
                                                    1-800-829-1040
   HIGHLAND HOPE UNITED METHODIST
     CHURCH
   23 TRILAND CT
   HIGHLAND  IL    62249                            OR WRITE TO THE ADDRESS
                                                    SHOWN AT THE TOP LEFT.

                                                    IF YOU WRITE, ATTACH THE
                                                    STUB OF THIS NOTICE.

            WE ASSIGNED YOU AN EMPLOYER IDENTIFICATION NUMBER (EIN)

       Thank you for your Form SS-4, Application for Employer Identification Number
  (EIN).  We assigned you EIN 37-1347190.  This EIN will identify your business account,
  tax returns, and documents, even if you have no employees.  Please keep this notice in
  your permanent records.

       Use your complete name and EIN shown above on all federal tax forms, payments,
  and related correspondence.  If you use any variation in your name or EIN, it may
  cause a delay in processing, incorrect information in your account, or cause you to be
  assigned more than one EIN.

       If you want to receive a ruling or a determination letter recognizing your
  organization as tax exempt, you should file Form 1023/1024, Application for
  Recognition of Exemption, with your IRS Key District office.  Publication 557, Tax
  Exempt Status for Your Organization, is available at most IRS offices and has details
  on how you can apply.

       Thank you for your cooperation.




                        Keep this part for your records.         CP 575 E (Rev. 1-95)
--------------------------------------------------------------------------------
       Return this part with any correspondence
       so we may identify your account.  Please                  CP 575 E
       correct any errors in your name or address.
                                                                 0916504651


       Your Telephone Number  Best Time to Call  DATE OF THIS NOTICE:  09-28-95
       (     )                                   EMPLOYER IDENTIFICATION NUMBER:  37-1347190
       _____       _____       FORM:  SS-4




       INTERNAL REVENUE SERVICE
       KANSAS CITY  MO    64999
                                                 HIGHLAND HOPE UNITED METHODIST
                                                   CHURCH
                                                 23 TRILAND CT
                                                 HIGHLAND  IL    62249
```

12. SAMPLE 501(c)3 IRS LETTER FOR TAX EXEMPTION

02/02/1996 10:52   618-242-9227   SO IL CONF UMC   PAGE 01

Illinois Department of Revenue

Legal Services Office, 5-500
101 W. Jefferson Street
Springfield, Illinois 62702

November 17, 1995

UNITED METHODIST CHURCH SOUTHERN IL CONFERENCE
DIR OF ADMINISTRATIVE SERVICES
1919 BROADWAY
MT VERNON IL 62864

We have received your recent letter; and based on the information you furnished, we believe

UNITED METHODIST CHURCH SOUTHERN IL CONFERENCE
of
MT VERNON, IL

is organized and operated exclusively for religious purposes.

Consequently, sales of any kind to this organization are exempt from the Retailers' Occupation Tax, the Service Occupation Tax (both state and local), the Use Tax, and Service Use Tax in Illinois. The organization is not, however, exempt from Illinois Hotel Operators' Occupation Tax.

We have issued your organization the following tax exemption identification number: E9989-8133-03. To claim the exemption, you must provide this number to your suppliers when purchasing tangible personal property for organizational use. This exemption may not be used by individual members of the organization to make purchases for their individual use.

This exemption will expire on December 1, 2000, unless you apply to the Illinois Department of Revenue for renewal at least three months prior to the expiration date.

Legal Services Office
Illinois Department of Revenue

Highland HOPE

STS-49 (N-1/95)
IL-492-3456

11~0000092

"Have an Answer for the Hope"
1 Peter 3:15

Rev. Troy D. Benitone
Church: (618) 654-8434 (Voice/Fax)   23 Triland Ct.
Home: (618) 654-4726   Highland, IL 62249

Appendix **145**

13. SAMPLE WORSHIP BULLETIN

Highland H♁PE

"Have An Answer for the Hope."
1 Peter 3:15

CHURCH OFFICE:
HIGHLAND HOPE
23 TRILAND COURT
HIGHLAND, ILLINOIS 62249

~

TELEPHONE: (618) 654-8434 (Voice/Fax)

~

Rev. Troy D. Benitone, Pastor
Connie Pellock, Administrative Assistant

A Developing Congregation of the United Methodist Church

13. SAMPLE WORSHIP BULLETIN
(CONTINUED)

"Celebrate the Hope"
January 5, 1997

ANNOUNCEMENTS & PRELUDE *A time for reflection & prayer*

~

CALL TO WORSHIP *"This is the Day"*
This is the day, this is the day that the Lord hath made, that the Lord hath made,
we will rejoice, we will rejoice and be glad in it, and be glad in it.
This is the day that the Lord hath made, we will rejoice and be glad in it.
This is the day, this is the day that the Lord hath made. **(REPEAT)** CCLI # 1070117

~

SONGS OF PRAISE MEDLEY
"My Life Is in You, Lord"
My life is in You, Lord, my strength is in You, Lord, my hope is in You,
Lord, in You, it's in You. My life is in You, Lord, my strength is in You,
Lord, my hope is in You, Lord, in You, it's in You.
I will praise You with all of my life, I will praise You with all of my strength;
with all of my life, with all of my strength, all of my hope is in You.
My life is in You, Lord, my strength is in You, Lord, my hope is in You,
Lord, in You, it's in You. My life is in You, Lord, my strength is in You,
Lord, my hope is in You, Lord, in You, it's in You, in You. CCLI # 1070117

"Lord, I Lift Your Name On High"
Lord, I lift Your name on high, Lord, I love to sing Your praises.
I'm so glad You're in my life, I'm so glad You came to save us.
You came from heaven to earth to show the way, from the earth to the cross,
my debt to pay; from the cross to the grave, from the grave to the sky;
Lord, I lift Your name on high. **(REPEAT)** CCLI # 1070117

"How Majestic Is Your Name"
O Lord, our Lord, how majestic is Your name in all the earth. O Lord, our Lord, how
majestic is Your name in all the earth. O Lord, we praise Your name. O Lord, we magnify
Your name, Prince of Peace, mighty God, O Lord God Almighty. **(REPEAT)** CCLI # 1070117

~

PASSING THE PEACE

KID'S KINGDOM SERMON
Following the Kid's Kingdom sermon all children PreK-6th grade are invited to attend the Kid's Kingdom program.

~

CONGREGATIONAL JOYS & CONCERNS
THE LORD'S PRAYER

Our Father, Who art in Heaven, hallowed be Thy name. Thy Kingdom come, Thy will be done on earth as it is in heaven. Give us this day our daily bread. And forgive us our trespasses, as we forgive those who trespass against us. And lead us not into temptation, but deliver us from evil. For Thine is the kingdom, and the power, and the glory, forever. ~Amen.

~

A GIFT OF HOPE - Offertory by Sheila Acuncius

~

HYMN OF HOPE - *"Spirit Song"*

O let the Son of God enfold you with his Spirit and his love.
Let him fill your heart and satisfy your soul. O let him have the things that hold you,
and his Spirit like a dove will descend upon your life and make you whole.

O come and sing this song with gladness as your hearts are filled with joy.
Lift your hands in sweet surrender to his name. O give him all your tears and sadness;
give him all your years of pain, and you'll enter into life in Jesus' name.

REFRAIN: Jesus, O Jesus, come and fill your lambs.
Jesus, O Jesus, come and fill your lambs. CCLI # 1070117

~

SERMON
SERIES: What's Happened to Christianity!

"A Personal Inventory!" - Rev. Troy D. Benitone, Pastor

Today's Scriptures
Luke 13: 6-9 (nkjv)

"He also spoke this parable: "A certain man had a fig tree planted in his vineyard, and he came seeking fruit on it and found none. *7 Then he said to the keeper of his vineyard, "Look, for three years I have come seeking fruit on this fig tree and find none. Cut it down; why does it use up the ground?" *8 But he answered and said to him, "Sir, let it alone this year also, until I dig around it and fertilize it. *9 And if it bears fruit, well. But if not, after that you can cut it down.""

13. SAMPLE WORSHIP BULLETIN (CONTINUED)

Romans 14: 11-12 (nkjv)
*"For it is written: "As I live, says the Lord, Every knee shall bow to Me, and every tongue shall confess to God." *12 So then each of us shall give account of himself to God.*

HYMN OF FAITH
"My Hope Is Built"

My hope is built on nothing less than Jesus' blood and righteousness.
I dare not trust the sweetest frame, but wholly lean on Jesus' name.

When darkness veils his lovely face, I rest on his unchanging grace.
In every high and stormy gale, my anchor holds within the veil.

When he shall come with trumpet sound, O may I then in him be found!
Dressed in his righteousness alone, faultless to stand before the throne!

REFRAIN: *On Christ the solid rock I stand, all other ground is sinking sand; all other ground is sinking sand.* CCLI #1070117

CONGREGATIONAL BENEDICTION
"The Trees of the Field"
(You Shall Go Out with Joy)

You shall go out with joy and be led forth with peace,
The mountains and the hills will break forth before you.
There'll be shouts of joy and all the trees of the field will clap,
will clap their hands. And all the trees of the field will clap their hands,
the trees of the field will clap their hands,
the trees of the field will clap their hands,
while you go out with joy. **(REPEAT)** CCLI #1070117

Ministers-All Christians, Pastor- Rev. Troy D. Benitone, Admin. Assistant- Connie Pellock, Keyboard- Sheila Acuncius, Pianist- Becky Laackmann, Announcements- Mark Winkler or Rick Acuncius, Song Leaders- Bob Oestringer, Julia Daniels & Karen Gurley, Sound System- Bryan Smith, Jay Schweickart & George Kampwerth, Nursery Staff- Lynn Middendorff, Tracy Schulte & Wendy Ringering, Kids Kingdom Staff - Konstance Kurrle - Coordinator & Teacher, Connie Pellock - Puppets Coordinator, Laura Pruett - Movie Sunday Coordinator, Julie Steinbruegge & Mary Dugan - Teachers

Appendix

UPCOMING EVENTS TO REMEMBER

Tuesday, Jan. 7 - **Office Team Crew** to meet @ 1:00pm at the Parsonage.

Sunday, Jan. 12 - **Boy Scout Pancake & Sausage Breakfast** serving 7:30am to 1:30pm at the KC Hall in Highland. All you can eat. Donation: Adults $4.50, Children $2.00, Under age 4 - Free.

Sunday, Jan. 12 - **Honduras Meeting** to discuss Honduras trip @ 5:00pm at the Parsonage.

Monday, Jan. 20 - **Martin Luther King Jr.'s Birthday**

Monday, Jan. 20 - **1997 All-Church Ski Trip** at Hidden Valley in St. Louis.

Tuesday, Feb. 4 - **Trustees Meeting** @ 7:00pm at the Parsonage.

BUILDING & DEVELOPMENT TASK TEAMS

Monday, Jan. 13 - **Interior Design & Landscape Teams** to meet @ 7:00pm at the Parsonage.

Sunday, Jan. 19 - **Capital Campaign Team** meeting @ 6:30pm at the Parsonage.

Tuesday, Jan. 21 - **Dream Team & Structure Teams** to meet @ 7:00pm at the Parsonage.

Thursday, Jan. 23 - **Dream Team & Structure Teams** to meet @ 7:00pm at the Parsonage.

Tuesday, Jan. 28 - **Dream Team & Structure Teams** to meet @ 7:00pm at the Parsonage.

Wednesday, Jan. 29 - **Dream Team & Structure Teams** to meet @ 7:00pm at the Parsonage.

Thursday, Jan. 30 - **Dream Team & Structure Teams** to meet @ 7:00pm at the Parsonage.

ON THE SIGN UP TABLE TODAY:
You can also sign up via the church ofc@ 654-8434

1. **YOUTH VOLLEYBALL LEAGUE:** Information about playing on an existing team or forming a new team is available at the sign-up table.

2. *1997 All-Church Ski Trip:* **Don' t miss your chance to assault Rev. Troy with snowballs!** We are planning a group trip to Hiddenvalley in St. Louis, on Monday, January 20 (Martin Luther King's Holiday) We will leave early in the morning, ski all day (9-4), eat dinner together and return home in the evening. (Cost: $30-$40 based on previous skiing experience) A sign-up sheet is in the foyer.

3. **Sound System Helpers:** Our sound system volunteers could use some additional help with setting up and taking down the sound system. If you would like to lend them a helping hand, a sign-up sheet is on the sign-up table today.

4. **Host family/individuals for Fellowship Sunday**: We plan to have a Fellowship Sunday once a month starting in January and continuing through May. The hosts will be responsible for bringing and serving a limited assortment of breakfast items to compliment the Coffee Service at our hospitality table. If you are interested in helping out with one or more Fellowship Sundays, please see the sign-up sheet at the table in the foyer.

13. SAMPLE WORSHIP BULLETIN (CONTINUED)

MINISTRY TEAM SCHEDULES FOR JANUARY

Nursery Care Team: Today - (Evelyn Bowers, Std by- Debbie Johnson)
1/12 - (Cassie Sherman, Std by- Kathryn Comish) 1/19 - (Debbie Missey, Std by-Debbie Johnson)
1/26 - (Dawn Davidson, Std by- Kathryn Comish)

Andrew Ministers:
Bull- Bulletin, T- Name Tags and Greeters table, Dr- Help with opening outer door for guests
Today - Jeff Johnson *(Dr)*, Ruth Rosenthal*(Bull)*, Sylvia Brandt & Charlotte Shaw*(T)*
1/12 (2nd Sun)-Erin & Joyce Remelius*(Bull)*, Laura Pruett & Connie Pellock*(T)*, Jason & Terry Remelius-*(Dr)*
1/19 (3rd Sun)- Gary Gurley *(Dr)*, Karen Gurley *(Bull)*, Debbie Missey *(T)*
1/26 (4th Sun)- Greg Bruning *(Dr)*, Sam Funkhouser *(Bull)*, Dianne Funkhouser*(T)*

To the Andrew Ministers & Ensemble members who are attending Christian Education classes:
You should plan to leave class a few minutes early in order to serve at your designated area.

SET-UP TEAM A: (January 5, 12, 19, 26) Start time is 8:30am

Heavy: Greg Bruning, Jim Fisher, Cevin Dugan   Driver: Jeff Johnson
Nursery: Cheryl Davidson, Kathryn Comish   Kid's Kingdom: Brenda Snowden, Connie Pellock
Greeters Area: Mary Dugan   Sd Sys: George Kampwerth, Chris Kurrle
Floater: Troy Benitone

PUPPET MINISTRY - All 4th, 5th, & 6th grade youth are invited to participate in this youth ministry. For more information about the puppet ministry program, please contact Connie Pellock @ 654-5759.
The next puppet practice is scheduled for Sat., Jan. 11, 10:30am - 11:30am at Connie Pellock's home.

YOUTH FOCUS WILL MEET TONIGHT AT THE PARSONAGE/BENITONE'S Meetings begin every Sunday at 5:30pm and run through 7:30pm. All Jr. & Sr. High Youth are invited to participate. For more information on our youth program or directions to the church parsonage, please contact Bryan or Tracy Smith at 644-3693.

WOMEN'S MINISTRIES AT HIGHLAND HOPE

PRAY & PLAY: MEETS ON WEDNESDAY MORNINGS FROM 10:00 TO NOON
Pray & Play is a ministry for stay-at-home mothers and fathers, who gather weekly for an hour of prayer & fellowship, while the children play. Karen Paubel is the coordinator and you can contact her at her home at 1723 Zschokke in Highland or call her at 654-5315, if you have any questions. This ministry is a good opportunity for you to invite friends that might be interested in Highland Hope. The January schedule is listed below.
Wednesday, Jan. 8 - Karen Paubel's home. The group will exchange ideas about indoor activities.
Wednesday, Jan. 22 - Karen Paubel's home. Experienced Moms will share secrets to raising happy children.

WOMEN'S BIBLE STUDY JANUARY SCHEDULE :
Tuesday, Jan. 14- @ 7:30pm at Karen Paubel's home. There will be a brief Bible Study of "How to Study the Bible" followed by a baby shower for Kathryn Comish. All the women of the church are invited to attend.
Tuesday, Jan. 28- @ 7:30pm at Karen Paubel's home.

A note of thanks to your generosity with the Highland Hope Adopt-A-Family for Christmas project. Thanks to your warmth and kindness, a family that wasn't expecting to have much of a Christmas was able to experience the joy of a very blessed Christmas.

14. RECIPE FOR CLASSIC ITALIAN BREAD

This recipe makes 2 large loaves, 6 mini loves or you can slice it to form multiple bread sticks.

INGREDIENTS:

2 packages fast-rising dry yeast

40 oz. (2½ cups) of lukewarm water (110 degrees is the best temperature for activating the yeast.)

2¼ lbs. of high-quality unbleached white bread flour (Do not use all-purpose flour.)

Make a salt solution with 1 tsp. salt dissolved in one tsp. of water

DIRECTIONS:

Mix the yeast in the lukewarm water, let sit for 5–6 minutes, then stir thoroughly to dissolve the yeast into the water. Make a batter by adding the yeast-water mix to about 4 cups of flour. Mix this for 10 minutes with an electric mixer. When it begins to pull away clean from the sides of the bowl, it is ready. Add the salt solution and the remaining flour. Knead using the dough hook attachment of a heavy-duty electric mixer or knead by hand for 10–15 minutes until thoroughly mixed. If the dough is still lumpy, work a little water in to help the flour break down to form a good dough ball.

Place the dough on a smooth surface or on a piece of plastic wrap and cover with a large bowl. Let rise for about 1½–2 hours or until it has doubled in size. Time will vary based on room temperature. Remove the bowl, punch down and turn in once, and let rise another 1½ hours. Punch it down again and separate into desired form (2 big loaves, several mini-loaves or bread sticks). Lay them on a cotton linen or cotton muslin cloth, sprinkle them with flour and cover them while you preheat your oven to 450 degrees. When the formed loaves have doubled in size they are ready for the oven. If you put a little corn meal on the baking surface the bread will slide on and off without sticking.

It's best to bake your bread on a baking stone. A pan of water in the oven will create a moist atmosphere in the oven which is the secret to curing the crust and making it hard-shelled but soft inside. Place loaves in the 450-degree oven on the stone or baking sheets and bake for 20–25 minutes depending on the loaf size.

The bread is done when it sounds hollow inside. Allow to cool on a rack and serve.

VARIATIONS:

If you like other things added to your bread—such as herbs, olives and other ingredients—simply add these toward the end of the kneading process. The bread is awesome when dipped in Extra Virgin Olive Oil and eaten.